First International Workshop on Knowledge-Enhanced Machine Translation (KEMT 2024)

Sheffield, United Kingdom
27 June 2024

ISBN: 979-8-3313-0480-5

Printed from e-media with permission by:

Curran Associates, Inc.
57 Morehouse Lane
Red Hook, NY 12571

CURRAN ASSOCIATES INC. proceedings.com

Some format issues inherent in the e-media version may also appear in this print version.

Association for Computational Linguistics
209 N. Eighth Street
Stroudsburg, Pennsylvania 18360

Phone: 1-570-476-8006
Fax: 1-570-476-0860

acl@aclweb.org

Additional copies of this publication are available from:

Curran Associates, Inc.
57 Morehouse Lane
Red Hook, NY 12571 USA
Phone: 845-758-0400
Fax: 845-758-2633
Email: curran@proceedings.com
Web: www.proceedings.com

KEMT

First International Workshop on Knowledge-Enhanced Machine Translation

Proceedings of the Workshop

June 27, 2024

The KEMT organizers gratefully acknowledge the support from the following sponsors.

Sponsors of the Workshop

GHENT UNIVERSITY

language and translation technology team

Introduction

This volume contains the proceedings of the First International Workshop on Knowledge-Enhanced Machine Translation (KEMT 2024), hosted by the 25th Annual Conference of the European Association for Machine Translation (EAMT 2024). KEMT 2024 focuses on all aspects of the integration of additional knowledge into machine translation, including translation memories, terminology, linguistic information, translation quality indicators ...
The workshop welcomed submissions of either research papers or extended abstracts/industry reports. Three research papers and two extended abstracts were received. Each submission was reviewed by three independent members of the program committee, and the final decision was made by the program chairs. The five submissions were accepted. The three research papers are to be presented orally, and the two extended abstracts will be presented as posters.
The accepted papers cover a diverse range of ways to add external information to machine translation systems: terminology, lexicons, fuzzy matches, hypernyms, and even language grammars.
In addition to the research papers and abstracts, we are honored to have two invited speakers from the industry: Ricardo Rei (Unbabel), with a keynote entitled "TowerLLM: Improving Translation Quality through Prompting with Terminology and Translation Guidelines"; and Tom Vanallemeersch (CrossLang) with the keynote "To Customize Is to Know: Leveraging In-house Knowledge for Multilingual Document Flows."
Finally, the program includes a panel discussion where participants can share their thoughts about many aspects of the integration of external information into machine translation: the needs of industry and trending research topics, how large language models are changing the landscape, etc.
We sincerely thank all the people and institutions that contributed to the success of the workshop: the authors of the submitted papers for their interest in the topic, the program committee members for their valuable feedback and insightful comments; and the EAMT organizers for their support. We also thank our sponsors, Ghent University and the Language and Translation Technology Team (LT3), for their generous contributions.

Arda Tezcan, Víctor M. Sánchez-Cartagena, Miquel Esplà-Gomis
Workshop Organizers

Organizing Committee

Members of the Organizing Committee and Program Chairs

Arda Tezcan, Universiteit Gent, Belgium
Víctor M. Sánchez-Cartagena, Universitat d'Alacant, Spain
Miquel Esplà-Gomis, Universitat d'Alacant, Spain

Program Committee

Program Committee

Frédéric Blain, Tilburg University, the Netherlands
Josep Crego, Systran, France
Miquel Esplà-Gomis, Universitat d'Alacant, Spain
Yasmin Moslem, Dublin City University, Ireland
Juan Antonio Pérez-Ortiz, Universitat d'Alacant, Spain
Víctor M. Sánchez-Cartagena, Universitat d'Alacant, Spain
Felipe Sánchez-Martínez, Universitat d'Alacant, Spain
Arda Tezcan, Universiteit Gent, Belgium
Torregrosa Torregrosa, World Intellectual Property Organization, Switzerland
Antonio Toral, University of Groningen, the Netherlands
Tom Vanallemeersch, CrossLang, Belgium
Vincent Vandeghinste, Instituut voor de Nederlandse Taal, the Netherlands
Bram Vanroy, Katholieke Universiteit Leuven, Belgium
François Yvon, CNRS and Sorbonne-Université, France

Invited Speakers

Ricardo Rei, Unbabel (Lisbon, Portugal)
Tom Vanallemeersch, CrossLang (Gent, Belgium)

Keynote Talk

To Customize Is to Know: Leveraging In-house Knowledge for Multilingual Document Flows

Tom Vanallemeersch
CrossLang (Gent, Belgium)
2024-06-27 09:05:00 – Room: **KEMT Workshop room**

Abstract: While the number of commercial and open-source multilingual NLP models steadily keeps growing, such generic models do not necessarily meet users' unique demands in full. This is especially true for companies and public administrations with highly specialized document flows. To optimize the use of multilingual tools, these organizations should be aware of the value of their in-house knowledge. This knowledge is not only embedded in multilingual assets like translation memories, documents in various languages and formats, or glossaries, but also the in-house expertise on document functionality and critical textual elements like terms and named entities.

Bio: Tom Vanallemeersch is Language AI Adviser at CrossLang, where he contributes to the customisation and deployment of multilingual NLP systems and coordinates the company's participation in publicly funded projects. Besides various positions in industry, including work at Systran, his career spans academia (PhD in computational linguistics at the University of Leuven) and consultancy for the European Commission (DG Translation's MT team). In his spare time, his membership of a chamber choir allows him to conduct multilingual experiments of a wholly different kind.

Keynote Talk

TowerLLM: Improving Translation Quality through Prompting with Terminology and Translation Guidelines

Ricardo Rei
Unbabel (Lisbon, Portugal)
2024-06-27 11:00:00 – Room: **KEMT Workshop room**

Abstract: TowerLLM revolutionizes machine translation by tailoring large language models (LLMs) to diverse translation tasks. By continued pretraining on mixed data and fine-tuning with task-specific instructions, TowerLLM surpasses open alternatives and rivals closed LLMs. This approach ensures proficiency across translation workflows, enhancing quality and efficiency. TowerLLM's impact extends beyond technical advancements, envisioning a future where specialized LLMs seamlessly integrate into translation pipelines, augmenting human capabilities. With the release of Tower models, specialized datasets, and evaluation frameworks, TowerLLM democratizes access to specialized resources, fostering collaboration and driving transformative advancements in machine translation.

Bio: Ricardo Rei is a senior research scientist at Unbabel, specializing in machine translation and natural language processing. He is set to complete his Ph.D. in April, which has been a collaborative effort between Unbabel, INESC-ID/Tecnico, and CMU University. His doctoral research has been centered on machine translation evaluation, and he is the main developer behind the COMET evaluation framework, which has become the industry standard metric for assessing machine translation quality. With a keen interest in advancing the capabilities of multilingual large language models (LLMs), he has been at the forefront of research and development in this domain. When not immersed in research, Ricardo enjoys maintaining an active lifestyle, often found at the gym or riding the waves while surfing—a passion he has pursued since the age of nine.

Table of Contents

Incorporating Hypernym Features for Improving Low-resource Neural Machine Translation

Abhisek Chakrabarty, Haiyue Song, Raj Dabre,
Hideki Tanaka, and **Masao Utiyama**
National Institute of Information and Communications Technology
3-5 Hikaridai, Seika-cho, Soraku-gun, Kyoto, 619-0289, Japan
{abhisek.chakra,haiyue.song,raj.dabre,hideki.tanaka,
mutiyama}@nict.go.jp

Abstract

Parallel data is difficult to obtain for low-resource languages in machine translation tasks, making it crucial to leverage monolingual linguistic features as auxiliary information. This article introduces a novel integration of hypernym features into the model by combining learnable hypernym embeddings with word embeddings, providing semantic information. Experimental results based on bilingual and multilingual models showed that: (1) incorporating hypernyms improves translation quality in low-resource settings, yielding +1.7 BLEU scores for bilingual models, (2) the hypernym feature demonstrates efficacy both in isolation and in conjunction with syntactic features, and (3) the performance is influenced by the choice of feature combination operators and hypernym-path hyperparameters.

1 Introduction

Low-resource neural machine translation (NMT) is an open challenge to NLP researchers because of a number of bottlenecks, such as a lack of parallel data and efficient linguistic tools, out-of-domain data, and morphological complexity of the languages. The majority of the research in this field either exploits monolingual and multilingual data in different ways (including back-translation (Edunov et al., 2018), transfer learning (Nguyen and Chiang, 2017; Song et al., 2020), and multilingual training (Dabre et al., 2020)) or come up with model-centric techniques for better modeling, training and inference (Haddow et al., 2022). Other than these two approaches, the use of linguistic knowledge is an effective strategy to improve translation quality under resource-scarce situations, however, relatively under-explored.

Linguistic analysis can be utilized for NMT both implicitly and explicitly. Implicit integration refers to methods that, instead of directly applying morphology into the model, use it as a part of pre-processing (subword segmentation of words based on legitimate units (Sánchez-Cartagena et al., 2020) or make a better contextual representation of the source sentence with the help of its syntactic/dependency structure (Eriguchi et al., 2016; Li et al., 2018; Bugliarello and Okazaki, 2020). In case of explicit use, either morphological information is included in the data to provide richer information about the source and the target languages (Sennrich and Haddow, 2016) or the model is trained with a multi-task objective to predict words along with their linguistic properties as secondary output (Luong et al., 2015) in order to obtain better internal word-form representation.

While morphological attributes are directly used in the source side as additional input features to words, it is hard to decide which input feature(s) are optimum to feed to the model for learning source-to-target mapping. Since the features are embedded in continuous space and can be combined easily, existing studies (Sennrich and Haddow, 2016; Chakrabarty et al., 2020; Chakrabarty et al., 2022) are found to use the following attributes together as supplementary components of a word - (1) part-of-speech (POS): tells syntactic behavior of individual words, (2) lemma: denotes base form and help to disambiguate inflectional variants, and (3) dependency parsing label:

Proceedings of the First International Workshop on Knowledge-Enhanced Machine Translation, pages 1–6
June 27, 2024 ©2024 European Association for Machine Translation

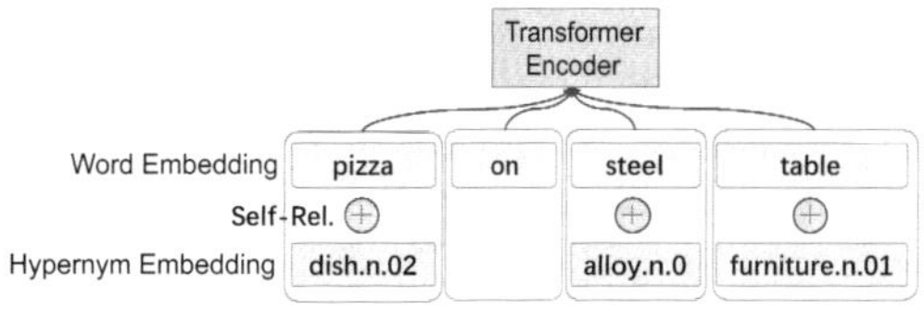

Figure 1: Incorporating hypernym features in the Encoder through Self-Relevance operation.

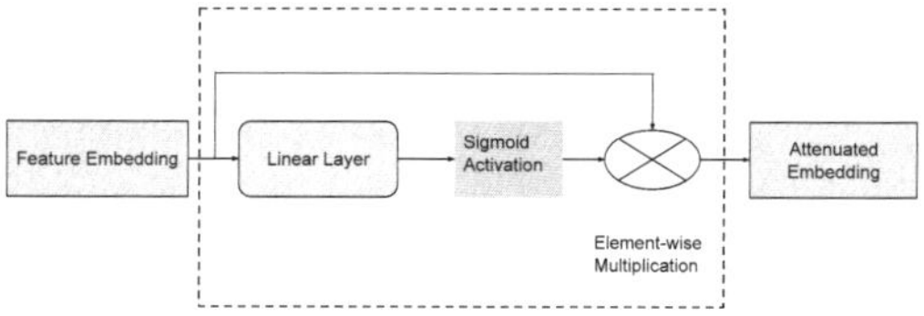

Figure 2: Self-relevance of a feature embedding.

provides the relationship with other words within a sentence. Although these three attributes are empirically established to help low-resource translation, however, they cannot impart distributional semantics which is crucial when there is not a sufficient amount of data available to learn linguistic regularities.

In this work, we try to address the above issue by incorporating hypernym information as a component of source words to meet the lack of distributional semantics in low-resource scenarios. As presented in Figure 1, hypernym provides superclass information, hence it can relate two distinct words with semantic similarity to some extent (e.g., *table* and *chair* in *furniture* sense) despite without any syntactic relation between them. One can argue that hypernym is an expensive knowledge typically obtained from WordNet (Miller, 1995) thus hardly available for low-resource languages. Nevertheless, building a primitive WordNet with hypernym relation is relatively easy and we aim to explore the potency of superclass information in NMT. In a nutshell, our contributions are as follows: (1) We incorporate hypernyms as a semantic component of word embeddings in low-resource MT, (2) Experimental results show BLEU score improvements from English to eight diverse low-resource Asian languages for both bilingual (+1.73 on avg.) and multilingual models (+0.24 on avg.), (3) We provide comparative analysis between syntactic vs. semantic feature combinations and hypernym-path hyperparameters variants.

2 Methodology

At first we provide the basics of two important concepts - how linguistic input features are used as additional components of a word in NMT models, and measuring the relevance of a feature embedding. Next, we describe the procedure of data annotation with hypernym information.

Linguistic Input Features into NMT: Sennrich and Haddow (2016) introduced a simple but effective way to incorporate linguistic input features into a word by concatenating word embedding and feature embeddings together. This approach supports an arbitrary number of features and enables the translation model to directly incorporate linguistic knowledge. In subword-based NMT, features corresponding to a word are replicated across its subwords. Given a source sentence s, if each of its token is represented with K features, then the ith token s_i can be denoted as $s_i = (s_{i1}, \ldots, s_{iK})$. Here, s_{i1} is the word or sub-word embedding, while $s_{i2}, \ldots, s_{iK}$ represent various linguistic features. For any feature type indexed by $k \in \{1, ..., K\}$, let V_k, E_k, and d_k be the vocabulary, embedding matrix and dimension of the embedded vector, respectively, with $E_k \in \mathbb{R}^{d_k \times |V_k|}$. The embedding of token s_i, denoted by e_i, can be computed as $\boldsymbol{e}_{ik} = E_k s_{ik}$, where $\boldsymbol{e}_{ik}$ is the embedding of s_{ik}. The final embedding for s_i is obtained as $\boldsymbol{e}_i = \|_{k=1}^{K} \boldsymbol{e}_{ik}$, where $\|$ signifies the concatenation operation.

Attenuating Feature Embeddings by Relevance: The above method by Sennrich and Haddow (2016) combines word and feature embeddings blindly and lacks to evaluate the functionality of a feature in terms of translation goal. Chakrabarty et al., (2020) claimed that providing extra morphological information may lead to noise when a word has only one sense. Hence, they came up with two strategies to attenuate feature embedding. The first one, named as *self-relevance*, measures the importance of a feature embedding w.r.t the embedding itself, and the second one, named as *word-based relevance*, considers both word and feature embeddings together to weight the feature embedding. Out of these two relevance mechanisms, Chakrabarty et al., (2020) empirically found self-relevance to be better. Hence, we use it throughout our experimentation and detail it as follows.

Self-Relevance: For the kth feature component s_{ik}, its embedded vector $\boldsymbol{e}_{ik}$ is transformed by a learnable weight matrix $W_k \in \mathbb{R}^{d_k \times d_k}$ followed by a sigmoid activation. It generates a mask vec-

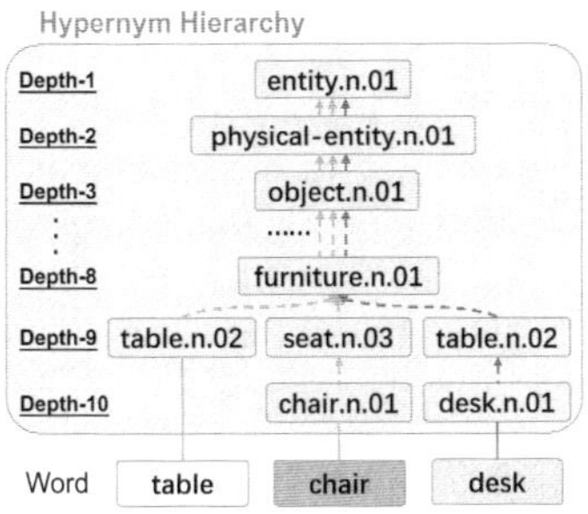

Figure 3: Depth-wise sense similarity of the synsets *table.n.02*, *chair.n.01*, and *desk.n.01*.

tor $mask_{ik}$ that contains the weight of $\mathbf{e}_{ik}$ as $mask_{ik} = \text{sigmoid}(W_k \mathbf{e}_{ik})$. Next, $\mathbf{e}_{ik}$ is element-wise multiplied by $mask_{ik}$ to modulate the relevance. The attenuated feature embedding is thus $\mathbf{e}'_{ik} = mask_{ik} \odot \mathbf{e}_{ik}$. Eventually all modified embeddings $\mathbf{e}'_{i1}, \ldots, \mathbf{e}'_{iK}$ are concatenated to form the source embedding $\mathbf{e}'_i = \|_{k=1}^{K} \mathbf{e}'_{ik}$ for token s_i. The process is depicted in Figure 2.

2.1 Hypernym as Additional Feature

As mentioned earlier, although there have been previous studies regarding the inclusion of several morphological attributes (POS, lemma, dependency labels, etc.) as the source word component for improving translation quality, no significant work has explored the potency of hypernym information for this purpose. Our effort is inspired by the recent work of (Bai et al., 2022) that builds a class-based language model to address context sparsity where words with common WordNet hypernyms are mapped to the same class. Inspired by this study, we hypothesize that hypernym as an input feature can alleviate the lack of distributional semantics in low-resource MT tasks.

We leverage WordNet (Miller, 1995) that defines a synset by grouping all related words together that uniquely represent one meaningful concept. It is a directed graph where nodes are synsets and the edges denote the relationships. Hypernymy conveys *[is-a]* relation between two synsets from superclass to subclass such as *furniture.n.01* $\rightarrow$ *table.n.02*. For two words, if there is a common hypernym in their respective hypernym-paths at a certain depth (from the root synset), it signifies their similarity at that depth. Figure 3 shows an example of three words 'table', 'chair', and 'desk' with their sense similarity at different depths obtained from hypernym-path information.

To annotate a word with hypernym, we follow the token-to-class mapping algorithm proposed by Bai et al., (2022) which uses the following constraints - (1) the word should have a noun synset, (2) the length of the hypernym-path should be longer than a minimum depth d, and (3) frequency of the word is less than a threshold frequency f. Bai et al., (2022) restricted to nouns because these are the most difficult class for language models to learn and hence, we also keep this constraint to annotate only those words that have at least one noun synset. A higher depth signifies deeper semantic matching and frequency filtering is applied to prevent function words. Words not satisfying the above points are tagged with *dummy* hypernym. Note that a word may present in multiple synsets corresponding to different senses and thus, it is very difficult to find the most appropriate hypernym-path for a given context. Therefore, we follow the standard strategy to iterate over the synsets in the order of sense frequency and choose the most frequent one following the depth constraint. It is safe not to set a large value of d to prevent a word annotated with inappropriate hypernym w.r.t its context.

3 Experimental Settings

Datasets: We chose Asian Language Treebank (ALT) (Riza et al., 2016) for our MT experiments, which is a multi-parallel MT dataset. The data is initially in English and translated into 12 Asian languages. Following the experimental settings of Chakrabarty et al., (2020), we fix English (en) as the source and eight Asian languages - Bengali (bg), Filipino (fi), Hindi (hi), Indonesian (id), Khmer (khm), Malay (ms), Myanmar (my) and Vietnamese (vi) as the targets. The size of the train/dev/test split for each language pair is $18,088/1,000/1,018$. In the bilingual setup, we trained eight separate NMT models for each direction, whereas in multilingual experiments, we trained a one-to-many NMT model from English to eight Asian languages. We use English as the source due to the availability of hypernyms and other morphological attributes.

Preprocessing: We apply Byte-Pair Encoding (BPE) (Sennrich et al., 2016) with 32k merge operations for subword segmentation. Multilingual setup identifies each target language by a special token appended at the source side. For English data, Stanford CoreNLP toolkit (Manning et al., 2014) is used to get POS, lemma, and dependency

ID	Features	d/f	Combination	en→bg	en→fi	en→hi	en→id	en→khm	en→ms	en→my	en→vi	Avg.
			Results of Bilingual Models									
1†	-	-	-	7.50	26.98	23.62	30.88	26.24	35.78	16.48	29.05	24.57
2	H	6/6k	Self-Rel	7.51	26.63	24.09	31.23	26.54	35.49	16.91	29.76	24.77
3	H	6/50k	Self-Rel	7.45	26.85	23.56	31.09	26.36	35.62	16.93	30.02	24.74
4	H	3/50k	Self-Rel	7.39	27.26	24.35	31.52	26.63	36.34	17.70	29.38	25.07
5†	PLD	-	Self-Rel	8.40	28.22	26.13	32.65	27.33	**37.22**	18.13	29.91	26.00
6	H+PLD	6/6k	Self-Rel	8.37	28.08	25.72	**32.70**	27.90	37.19	**18.64**	31.30	26.24
7	H+PLD	6/50k	Self-Rel	**8.44**	**28.64**	**26.24**	32.68	27.83	36.80	18.46	31.29	**26.30**
8	H+PLD	3/50k	Self-Rel	8.35	28.17	26.05	32.44	**28.17**	36.71	18.52	**31.63**	26.25
9	H+PLD	6/50k	Concat	8.22	27.42	24.88	31.48	27.18	36.41	17.69	30.52	25.48
			Results of Multilingual Models									
	Features	d/f	Combination	en→bg	en→fi	en→hi	en→id	en→khm	en→ms	en→my	en→vi	Avg.
10†	-	-	-	11.55	31.04	27.29	34.78	30.27	39.37	20.93	34.58	28.73
11	H	6/6k	Self-Rel	11.44	31.70	27.82	35.12	30.45	**39.95**	20.88	34.34	28.96
12	H	6/50k	Self-Rel	11.56	31.63	27.24	35.18	30.51	39.55	21.01	34.48	28.90
13	H	3/50k	Self-Rel	**11.67**	**31.77**	26.95	**35.50**	30.20	39.64	21.06	34.50	28.91
14†	PLD	-	Self-Rel	11.40	31.14	27.94	34.42	30.09	39.84	20.99	33.85	28.71
15	H+PLD	6/6k	Self-Rel	11.36	31.08	27.91	34.76	30.78	38.79	21.10	34.13	28.74
16	H+PLD	6/50k	Self-Rel	11.52	30.96	**28.52**	34.54	30.84	38.83	21.17	34.60	28.87
17	H+PLD	3/50k	Self-Rel	11.50	30.92	28.15	35.14	**31.08**	39.13	**21.30**	34.57	**28.97**
18	H+PLD	3/50k	Concat	11.22	30.60	27.47	34.50	30.68	38.86	21.13	**34.62**	28.66

Table 1: BLEU scores of bilingual and multilingual models. 'H', 'P', 'L', 'D' refer to hypernym, POS, lemma, and dependency tag, respectively. d and f refer to the minimum depth of hypernym-path and maximum word frequency, respectively. Line with † stands for results reported in (Chakrabarty et al., 2022).

tags as lexical and syntactic features,. Additionally, subword tag (Sennrich et al., 2016) is used as a positional feature for each subword.

Hypernym Annotation: We use WordNet (Miller, 1995) to annotate the data with hypernyms. As there is no straightforward way to find the optimum values of a minimum depth of the hypernym-path and threshold to maximum frequency of a word, we start with the standard combination of $d/f = 6/6k$ used by Bai et al., (2022). Next, we try with two other combinations: (1) $6/50k$: which does not restrict words based on frequency but prioritizes content words, and (2) $3/50k$: mapping distant words together, permitting shallower semantic matching. By setting $d = 6$, we get $1,502$ distinct synsets in the annotated data.

Hyperparameters and Training Details: We use Transformer-base model (Vaswani et al., 2017) with the standard set of hyperparameters of 6 layers, 8 attention-heads, $2,048$ as fully-connected-feed-forward dimension, $8,000$ warmup steps, Adam optimizer (Kingma and Ba, 2015), $4,096$ tokens as batch size. Dropout tuning is found to be sensitive and hence, varied from 0.1-0.4. The final token embedding dimension is set to 512 across all models to make the parameters comparable. Inference is done using beam size 5. BLEU score (Papineni et al., 2002) is used for evaluation.

4 Results

Table 1 presents the bilingual and multilingual translation results in the order of - (1) without any feature, (2) with hypernym as semantic feature (H), (3) with POS, lemma, and dependency tag (PLD) as lexical and syntactic features, and (4) all features together (H+PLD), with different hypernym-path hyperparameters and combination approaches.

Bilingual Models: Compared with the baseline model without using any feature, incorporating hypernyms showed up to 0.50 avg. BLEU improvement (ID 1 vs. ID 4). While using other linguistic knowledge also proves to be effective ($+1.43$ avg. BLEU comparing ID 1 with ID 5), combining hypernym with PLD yielded the best avg. BLEU score of 26.30 (ID 7). This proved that the hypernym feature is complementary to syntactic features in a bilingual setup. We performed statistical significance tests on individual language pairs between IDs - $(2, 6)$, $(3, 7)$ and $(4, 8)$ and found results statistically significant with $p < 0.05$ for all language pairs.

Multilingual Models: It is evident from Table 1

that multilingual training showed better translation quality than bilingual training across all language pairs because of knowledge sharing over eight language pairs. Chakrabarty et al., (2022) found that in a multilingual scenario, the inclusion of morphological attributes cannot improve over the base model (ID 14 vs. ID 10) as linguistic regularities are learned from the data itself. However, we distinctly observed the importance of adding hypernyms by comparing ID 10 vs. 11. A significant performance gain is observed for en→fi, en→hi, and en→ms directions with $p < 0.05$. Additionally, we did not obtain remarkable improvement when combining all features suggesting that in a multilingual setup, proving hypernym feature is the more helpful one.

Hypernym Hyperparameters: To determine the optimal d/f combination, we analyze the results where only hypernyms are used (IDs $2, 3, 4$ and $11, 12, 13$ for bilingual and multilingual setups, respectively). For bilingual models, $d/f = 3/50k$ (ID 4) produced the best avg. BLEU as well the best scores for en→fi, en→hi, en→id, en→khm, en→my, and en→my translation directions. For multilingual models, all three combinations (IDs $11, 12, 13$) performed equally well. Therefore, we further analyze where all features are used (IDs $15, 16, 17$) and find that 3/50k is the optimal combination for both settings, showing that shallow semantic annotation is better.

Feature Combinations: As throughout our bilingual and multilingual experiments from IDs $2 - 8, 11 - 17$, the self-relevance technique is selected for embedding combination, we further investigate the performance of simple concatenation of word and feature embeddings (Sennrich et al., 2016) and present the results in IDs 9 and 18, clearly showing the superiority of self-relevance.

Training Curves: Figure 4 shows the initial training plots for bilingual (en→khm) and multilingual models. Adding hypernyms slows training in every configuration but using PLD features speeds up the convergence. Validation perplexity becomes stable after around $8k$ batches but we continue training to note that longer training improves validation BLEU scores significantly. In our experiments, after $60k$ and $100k$ training steps for bilingual and multilingual models respectively, we did not observe further improvements in BLEU, proving that perplexity drop does not always correlate with BLEU gain.

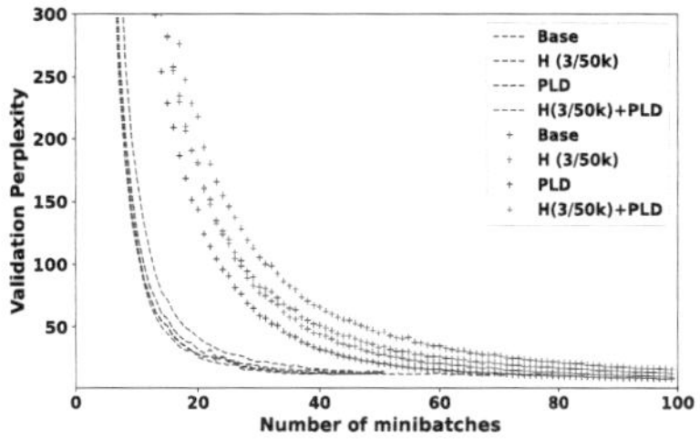

Figure 4: Bilingual (- - -) and multilingual (+) plots.

5 Conclusion

This study investigates the role of hypernyms used as a word embedding component to exploit distributional semantics in low-resource settings. Experiments over eight language pairs reveal its usefulness strongly in bilingual scenarios. We also conducted one-to-many multilingual experiments finding the superiority of semantic feature over lexical and syntactic features. We analyze training plots to show that perplexity drop is not always a good measure to evaluate model training. The future extension of this work will include - (1) finding the most appropriate hypernym-path of a contextual word, and (2) determining the optimum combination of semantic and syntactic features to leverage linguistic knowledge for low-resource translation.

References

Bai, He, Tong Wang, Alessandro Sordoni, and Peng Shi. 2022. Better language model with hypernym class prediction. In *Proceedings of the 60th Annual Meeting of the Association for Computational Linguistics (Volume 1: Long Papers)*, pages 1352–1362, Dublin, Ireland, May. Association for Computational Linguistics.

Bugliarello, Emanuele and Naoaki Okazaki. 2020. Enhancing machine translation with dependency-aware self-attention. In *Proceedings of the 58th Annual Meeting of the Association for Computational Linguistics*, pages 1618–1627, Online, July. Association for Computational Linguistics.

Chakrabarty, Abhisek, Raj Dabre, Chenchen Ding, Masao Utiyama, and Eiichiro Sumita. 2020. Improving low-resource NMT through relevance based linguistic features incorporation. In *Proceedings of the 28th International Conference on Computational Linguistics*, pages 4263–4274, Barcelona, Spain (Online), December. International Committee on Computational Linguistics.

Chakrabarty, Abhisek, Raj Dabre, Chenchen Ding,

Hideki Tanaka, Masao Utiyama, and Eiichiro Sumita. 2022. FeatureBART: Feature based sequence-to-sequence pre-training for low-resource NMT. In *Proceedings of the 29th International Conference on Computational Linguistics*, pages 5014–5020, Gyeongju, Republic of Korea, October. International Committee on Computational Linguistics.

Dabre, Raj, Chenhui Chu, and Anoop Kunchukuttan. 2020. A survey of multilingual neural machine translation. *ACM Comput. Surv.*, 53(5), September.

Edunov, Sergey, Myle Ott, Michael Auli, and David Grangier. 2018. Understanding back-translation at scale. In *Proceedings of the 2018 Conference on Empirical Methods in Natural Language Processing*, pages 489–500, Brussels, Belgium, October-November. Association for Computational Linguistics.

Eriguchi, Akiko, Kazuma Hashimoto, and Yoshimasa Tsuruoka. 2016. Tree-to-sequence attentional neural machine translation. In *Proceedings of the 54th Annual Meeting of the Association for Computational Linguistics (Volume 1: Long Papers)*, pages 823–833, Berlin, Germany, August. Association for Computational Linguistics.

Haddow, Barry, Rachel Bawden, Antonio Valerio Miceli Barone, Jindřich Helcl, and Alexandra Birch. 2022. Survey of low-resource machine translation. *Computational Linguistics*, 48(3):673–732, September.

Kingma, Diederik and Jimmy Ba. 2015. Adam: A method for stochastic optimization. In *International Conference on Learning Representations (ICLR)*, San Diega, CA, USA.

Li, Qiang, Derek F. Wong, Lidia S. Chao, Muhua Zhu, Tong Xiao, Jingbo Zhu, and Min Zhang. 2018. Linguistic knowledge-aware neural machine translation. *IEEE/ACM Trans. Audio, Speech and Lang. Proc.*, 26(12):2341–2354, December.

Luong, Minh-Thang, Quoc V. Le, Ilya Sutskever, Oriol Vinyals, and Lukasz Kaiser. 2015. Multi-task sequence to sequence learning. *CoRR*, abs/1511.06114.

Manning, Christopher D., Mihai Surdeanu, John Bauer, Jenny Finkel, Steven J. Bethard, and David McClosky. 2014. The Stanford CoreNLP natural language processing toolkit. In *Association for Computational Linguistics (ACL) System Demonstrations*, pages 55–60.

Miller, George A. 1995. Wordnet: A lexical database for english. *Commun. ACM*, 38(11):39–41, nov.

Nguyen, Toan Q. and David Chiang. 2017. Transfer learning across low-resource, related languages for neural machine translation. In *Proceedings of the Eighth International Joint Conference on Natural Language Processing (Volume 2: Short Papers)*, pages 296–301, Taipei, Taiwan, November. Asian Federation of Natural Language Processing.

Papineni, Kishore, Salim Roukos, Todd Ward, and Wei-Jing Zhu. 2002. Bleu: a method for automatic evaluation of machine translation. In *Proceedings of the 40th Annual Meeting of the Association for Computational Linguistics*, pages 311–318, Philadelphia, Pennsylvania, USA, July. Association for Computational Linguistics.

Riza, Hammam, Michael Purwoadi, Gunarso, Teduh Uliniansyah, Aw Ai Ti, Sharifah Mahani Aljunied, Luong Chi Mai, Vu Tat Thang, Nguyen Phuong Thai, Rapid Sun, Vichet Chea, Khin Mar Soe, Khin Thandar Nwet, Masao Utiyama, and Chenchen Ding. 2016. https://ieeexplore.ieee.org/document/7918974/ Introduction of the Asian language treebank. In *Proc. of O-COCOSDA*, pages 1–6.

Sánchez-Cartagena, Víctor M., Juan Antonio Pérez-Ortiz, and Felipe Sánchez-Martínez. 2020. Understanding the effects of word-level linguistic annotations in under-resourced neural machine translation. In *Proceedings of the 28th International Conference on Computational Linguistics*, pages 3938–3950, Barcelona, Spain (Online), December. International Committee on Computational Linguistics.

Sennrich, Rico and Barry Haddow. 2016. Linguistic input features improve neural machine translation. In *Proceedings of the First Conference on Machine Translation: Volume 1, Research Papers*, pages 83–91, Berlin, Germany, August. Association for Computational Linguistics.

Sennrich, Rico, Barry Haddow, and Alexandra Birch. 2016. Neural machine translation of rare words with subword units. In *Proceedings of the 54th Annual Meeting of the Association for Computational Linguistics (Volume 1: Long Papers)*, pages 1715–1725, Berlin, Germany, August. Association for Computational Linguistics.

Song, Haiyue, Raj Dabre, Zhuoyuan Mao, Fei Cheng, Sadao Kurohashi, and Eiichiro Sumita. 2020. Pre-training via leveraging assisting languages for neural machine translation. In *Proceedings of the 58th Annual Meeting of the Association for Computational Linguistics: Student Research Workshop*, pages 279–285, Online, July. Association for Computational Linguistics.

Vaswani, Ashish, Noam Shazeer, Niki Parmar, Jakob Uszkoreit, Llion Jones, Aidan N Gomez, Ł ukasz Kaiser, and Illia Polosukhin. 2017. Attention is all you need. In Guyon, I., U. V. Luxburg, S. Bengio, H. Wallach, R. Fergus, S. Vishwanathan, and R. Garnett, editors, *Advances in Neural Information Processing Systems 30*, pages 5998–6008. Curran Associates, Inc.

Exploring Inline Lexicon Injection for Cross-Domain Transfer in Neural Machine Translation

Jesujoba O. Alabi*
Saarland University, Germany
jalabi@lsv.uni-saarland.de

Rachel Bawden
Inria, Paris, France
rachel.bawden@inria.fr

Abstract

Domain transfer remains a challenge in machine translation (MT), particularly concerning rare or unseen words. Amongst the strategies proposed to address the issue, one of the simplest and most promising in terms of generalisation capacity is coupling the MT system with external resources such as bilingual lexicons and appending inline annotations within source sentences. This method has been shown to work well for controlled language settings, but its usability for general language (and ambiguous) MT is less certain. In this article we explore this question further, testing the strategy in a multi-domain transfer setting for German-to-English MT, using the mT5 language model fine-tuned on parallel data. We analyse the MT outputs and design evaluation strategies to understand the behaviour of such models. Our analysis using distractor annotations suggests that although improvements are not systematic according to automatic metrics, the model does learn to select appropriate translation candidates and ignore irrelevant ones, thereby exhibiting more than a systematic copying behaviour. However, we also find that the method is less successful in a higher-resource setting with a larger lexicon, suggesting that it is not a magic solution, especially when the baseline model is already exposed to a wide range of vocabulary.

1 Introduction

Data-driven machine translation (MT) models, and in particular neural MT models, have led to significant progress in the quality of automatic translation, particularly in settings where large amounts of data are available (Barrault et al., 2020; Akhbardeh et al., 2021; Saunders, 2021). However, a scenario in which MT typically struggles to perform as well is cross-domain transfer (Koehn and Knowles, 2017; Vu et al., 2021; Pham et al., 2021; Hasler et al., 2021; Bogoychev and Chen, 2021), where a model trained on one domain is adapted to a second domain, for which there typically exists less data. A major challenge is ensuring that the model is capable of handling the domain-specific vocabulary of the new domain, which may be rare or even unseen in the initial training corpus (Hu et al., 2019).

Domain adaptation for MT has benefited from pretraining via language models (Devlin et al., 2019; Lample and Conneau, 2019; Liu et al., 2020) trained on large quantities of monolingual text, therefore exposing the model to a wider vocabulary and improving cross-domain transfer (Clinchant et al., 2019; Verma et al., 2022). However, the model's capacity to exploit this underlying vocabulary is limited by the problem of catastrophic forgetting (Goodfellow et al., 2013) after fine-tuning (Hasler et al., 2021; Arthaud et al., 2021); the model becomes overly specific to the new data and loses the capacity to generalise to new domains.

A line of research with the aim of tackling this problem is the use of external resources such as bilingual lexicons and dictionaries (Tan et al., 2015; Dinu et al., 2019). These resources, comprising words or phrases and their translations (or words and their definitions in the case of dictionaries) provide a wider (and complementary) lexical coverage than the parallel training data. One aim is for the trained model to be able to exploit the external resource whenever a domain-specific or rare word appears. Different integration strategies have been proposed, including interpolation of translation probabilities and external lexicon probabilities (Arthur et al., 2016), the use of memory networks

*Work done at Inria, Paris, France

Proceedings of the First International Workshop on Knowledge-Enhanced Machine Translation, pages 7–20
June 27, 2024 ©2024 European Association for Machine Translation

(Feng et al., 2017), constrained decoding (Hasler et al., 2018), and the inclusion of inline information such as translation candidates (Dinu et al., 2019; Pham et al., 2018; Niehues, 2021) and definitions (Zhong and Chiang, 2020).

In this work, we explore the last of these strategies: attaching additional information inline within the source sentence as a way of incorporating domain-specific translation knowledge. It is a simple and commonly used method in the literature and one that has been shown to work well in controlled language settings (i.e. where terms are known in advance and can be translated without ambiguity) (Dinu et al., 2019). Our aim is to explore how this strategy could work in a practical setting for cross-domain adaptation in the general translation setting, particularly when using pretrained language models that have seen a wider variety of vocabulary than those trained just on parallel data (the previous studies concentrate on vanilla MT). We try to gain some insights into how inline information is used, whether models are able to generalise, disambiguate between multiple candidate translations and how this can ultimately help cross-domain transfer. Our experiments on German-to-English (de→en) translation show that the use of the method in this more general (as opposed to controlled) setting is not so successful. Our results are largely negative; we can see small (although not systematic) improvements when applying a model to a new domain. However, we also analyse how the approach works; through a systematic analysis, we show that the approach is more than just a copy mechanism, as we see evidence for the inline translation candidates being used effectively by the model, even when distractor candidates are introduced. We also show that in a higher-resource setting with a more diverse training vocabulary and a larger lexicon, the method is less effective and therefore it is not a go-to method in all settings. Our code and outputs will be made publicly available.

2 Related Work

Different strategies exploiting bilingual lexicons and dictionaries have been developed in the past to handle rare words, the majority focusing on integrating bilingual lexicons containing word (or phrase) translation pairs (Song et al., 2019; Dinu et al., 2019; Duan et al., 2020). They differ from normal parallel data in that entries are shorter and they often cover domain-specific and rare vocabulary.

These strategies include but are not limited to adding lexicons to the parallel training data (Tan et al., 2015), combining translation and external lexicon probabilities (Arthur et al., 2016), using memory networks (Feng et al., 2017), constrained decoding (Hasler et al., 2018) and infixing of translation candidates within the source sentence (Pham et al., 2018; Dinu et al., 2019; Michon et al., 2020; Niehues, 2021). In this inline approach, the idea is to either add translations inline within the source sentences or to replace the terms with their translations. It has been shown to work well with controlled and non-ambiguous settings (Dinu et al., 2019; Niehues, 2021) and when using a mechanism to encourage annotation copying (Pham et al., 2018). A similar code-switching-inspired method was introduced by Song et al. (2019), whereby terms are replaced by their translations from bilingual lexicons, and the generated examples used as extra training data. Xu and Yvon (2021) also look at code-switched data, replacing terms with their translation equivalents. Similar strategies have been used elsewhere, for example Duan et al. (2020) integrate code-switching-style replacements using the bilingual lexicon in the back-translation step of an unsupervised MT model, and Junczys-Dowmunt and Grundkiewicz (2016) and Crego et al. (2016) augment sentences with fuzzy translation matches.

A few studies have looked into the use of dictionary definitions in MT, as opposed to bilingual lexicons. Zhong and Chiang (2020) use a method similar to Dinu et al. (2019), involving appending unknown words' definitions to source sentences and indicating through positional embeddings to which words the definitions are attached. Beyond MT, the use of dictionary definitions has also been investigated for word embedding creation: Bosc and Vincent (2018) by auto-encoding and reconstructing definitions to improve word embeddings and Shi et al. (2019) by using definitions as a bridge between translations. Theoretically, there is not a clear distinction between bilingual lexicons and bilingual dictionaries in that dictionary definitions often contain synonyms (corresponding to translations in the bilingual case). However, we would expect dictionary definitions to be descriptive rather than translations.[1] In this work, we use bilingual lexicons (containing possible translate candidates)

[1]A number of works (Arthur et al., 2016; Pham et al., 2018) use automatically constructed phrase tables as lexicons, which differ in that they often contain noisy candidates and many inflections, whereas lexicons are often restricted to lemmas.

rather than dictionaries, but where several possible candidates are present for each source word.

3 Integrating Lexicon Entries

We concentrate on the use of bilingual lexicons with word-candidate pairs to improve domain transfer in MT. Some examples of the bilingual lexicon entries are given in Table 1. Many of the entries contain a single translation for each term, but some of the terms have several possible translation candidates.

German term	English translation(s)
verehren	to carry a torch for [Am.] to adore, to enshrine, to revere, to venerate
wut	angriness, furiousness, fury, irateness, rabidness, rage, wrath
wälzlager	antifriction bearing, rolling contact bearing
biologisch abbaubar	biodegradable
tuberkulös	tuberculous

Table 1: Examples of bilingual lexicon entries.

Specifically, we consider a scenario where we train MT models to translate from German to English and attempt to transfer them to new domains by incorporating bilingual lexicon entries inline within source sentences (Pham et al., 2018; Dinu et al., 2019; Zhong and Chiang, 2020; Niehues, 2021).[2] We compare this to an alternative strategy, which is to concatenate the bilingual lexicon to the training data, i.e. treating it as additional parallel data, with the advantage that the entire lexicon can be used for training (rather than only the words that appear in the training data) but with the disadvantage that the method cannot generalise to novel lexicon entries.[3] In this sense, it may be seen as a model included for results comparison, but not one which could be considered a desirable alternative.

3.1 `inline`: Infixing Lexicon Entries within Source Sentences

We use the bilingual lexicon to provide context during training and at inference time for unknown or rare words. We do this by annotating identified terms in the source sentence with their corresponding target entries. For every word in the data that appears fewer than k times in the training data (i.e. the data on which the pretrained language model is fine-tuned),[4] we search for a corresponding lexicon entry to append inline to the term. Contrarily to (Niehues, 2021) and as in (Zhong and Chiang, 2020), we choose not to disambiguate the translation candidates and simply add the raw entry inline so that the model can learn to choose the most appropriate translation, potentially more appropriate in non-controlled language setting. Entries therefore resemble dictionary entries. An example of a German source sentence augmented with lexicon entries is shown in Example 1, with two rare words (underlined) and their translations according to the lexicon added within `<def></def>` tags.[5]

(1) **German source**: Begleittherapie Timolol kann mit anderen <u>Arzneimitteln</u> <def>pharmacotherapy</def> <u>wechselwirken</u> <def>interactively</def> (siehe Abschnitt 4.5)
English reference: Concomitant therapy Timolol may interact with other medicinal products (see section 4.5).

In order to expand the lookup in the lexicon beyond exact token matches,[6] we match rare words with lexicon terms by choosing the one with the shortest normalised Levenshtein distance. Similar to (Zhong and Chiang, 2020), to make this computation more efficient (by reducing the search space over the lexicon), we use locality-sensitive hashing (LSH) by creating vectors of all the lexicon headwords using their character-level trigrams. The rare words are then queried against the lexicon using the Jaccard[7] score character-level trigram overlap. The rare words that do not meet the Jaccard threshold will have no annnotation attached to them.

Including translations inline gives the model the potential to handle new entries. However, its main disadvantage is an increase in source sentence length, which can be problematic for models whose maximum sentence length is small.

3.2 `concat`: Using Bilingual Lexicons as Parallel Training Data

We compare this to the method of mixing the bilingual lexicon into the parallel training data. We consider two versions (see examples in Table 2): (i) `concat-diff`: mixing the data sources and prefixing each training instance with a different tag

[2]Unlike Pham et al. (2018), we do not force the model to copy the annotations and instead choose to explore the scenario where the model can learn to copy if relevant.

[3]Alternative fine-tuning strategies for continual learning would have to be used (Arthaud et al., 2021).

[4]A word is defined here as a token as obtained by the Moses tokeniser (Koehn et al., 2007).

[5]Note that, as shown in this example, the candidate translations do not always correspond to the reference translation. However, they may nevertheless provide lexical knowledge enabling the model to make a correct translation choice.

[6]We leave the multi-token matching to future work.

[7]We use a Jaccard similarity threshold score of 0.7.

Data	concat	concat-diff
Lexicon	**src**: transDeEn: beleuchtungstechnik **ref**: lighting technology	**src**: defDeEn: beleuchtungstechnik **ref**: lighting technology
Parallel	**src**: transDeEn: Schlucken Sie die Kapsel(n) als Ganzes mit einem Glas Wasser. **ref**: Swallow the capsule(s) whole with a glass of water.	**src**: transDeEn: Schlucken Sie die Kapsel(n) als Ganzes mit einem Glas Wasser. **ref**: Swallow the capsule(s) whole with a glass of water.

Table 2: `concat` strategy: mixing the two data sources (lexicon and parallel) without distinguishing their origin (`concat`) and with different tags indicating the data source (`concat-diff`).

indicating the data source and (i) `concat`: mixing the two data sources together without distinguishing the two sources. The hypothesis is that this could help the model distinguish the two data types as previously seen for domain labels (Kobus et al., 2017; Caswell et al., 2019) and politeness (Sennrich et al., 2016). Note that in practice, we use the prefix `tranDeEn:` for source sentences of all models (including `inline`), except for `concat-diff`, where the prefix `defDeEn:` is used for lexicon entries.

4 Experimental Setup

4.1 Data

Training Data We cover four different domains: biomedical, commerce, news and films, using data from EMEA,[8] ECB,[9] GlobalVoices,[10] and OpenSubtitles2018[11] (Lison et al., 2018) from OPUS (Tiedemann, 2012). Pre-processing includes fixing orthographic errors, removing duplicate parallel sentences, and filtering via language identification with Bifixer/Bicleaner (Sánchez-Cartagena et al., 2018; Ramírez-Sánchez et al., 2020) and FastText (Joulin et al., 2016; Joulin et al., 2017). Table 3 shows the dataset sizes after pre-processing.

Source	Domain	Train	Dev.	Test
GlobalVoices	news	~ 61k	2k	2k
ECB	commerce	~76k	2k	2k
EMEA	medical	~235k	2k	2k
Opensubtitles	movies	~16M	2k	2k
WMT				
$News_{18}$	news	–	–	2998
$News_{20}$	news	–	–	785
$News_{22}$	news	–	–	506
$Medline_{20}$	medical	–	–	404
$eCom_{22}$	commerce	–	–	501
Soc_{22}	social	–	–	515
$Conv_{22}$	conversation	–	–	462

Table 3: #sentences per dataset per domain.

Validation and Test Data From each dataset, we split off distinct 2000 random sentence pairs from the pre-processed data for each of the validation and test sets. We also test on other datasets: the WMT 2018 and 2020 news test sets, the WMT 2018 biomedical test set and the different genres from the 2022 WMT General MT task: news, e-commerce, social, and chat (see Table 3).

Bilingual Lexicon We use the Stardict German-English dictionary (based on Freedict[12] and originally with 81,628 entries). We preprocess the lexicon by removing empty entries, lower-casing German headwords, concatenating multiple candidates of a same headword, and deleting bracketed descriptions. The final lexicon has 79,936 entries (German headwords) associated with one or more English translations (see examples of the preprocessed entries in Table 1). In `concat` approaches (treating the lexicon as parallel data), we filter out 150 lexicon entries to use as a development set.

4.2 Training Setup

We initialise all MT models using the pre-trained multilingual language model mT5-base (Xue et al., 2021), implemented in Transformers (Wolf et al., 2020).[13] We train the models for up to 40 epochs with a batch size of 10, a learning rate of 5e-5, dropout of 0.1, and a maximum source and target length of 512. For decoding, we use a beam of 10. The output of the best checkpoint (according to the training loss) is evaluated using BLEU (Papineni et al., 2002) as computed by SacreBLEU[14] (Post, 2018). We choose to use BLEU for evaluation because we observe similar trends with other metrics such as COMET (Rei et al., 2020), and BLEU has the advantage of having more easily interpretable

[8] European Medicines Agency: `https://www.ema.europa.eu`

[9] European Central Bank: `https://www.ecb.europa.eu`

[10] GlobalVoices: `https://globalvoices.org`

[11] `https://www.opensubtitles.org`

[12] `https://freedict.org/`

[13] `https://github.com/huggingface/transformers`

[14] `case:mixed|eff:no| tok:13a|smooth:exp|v:2.3.1`

Setup	EMEA	ECB	GV	News18	News20	Med20	News22	eCom22	Soc22	Conv22
Trained on Globalvoices										
Baseline	**21.1**	**19.2**	32.0	33.5	23.4	24.5	**22.3**	22.3	**23.1**	23.8
`concat-diff`	20.6	18.9	31.7	33.5	23.2	**24.6**	21.5	22.8	21.8	**24.0**
`concat`	20.6	19.1	31.6	33.1	23.4	24.2	21.5	22.8	22.0	23.9
`inline`	20.9	18.8	**32.1**	**33.7**	**24.1**	24.5	21.8	22.7	22.8	23.8
`inline+concat-diff`	20.5	18.6	31.7	33.2	23.2	24.2	21.5	**23.1**	21.9	23.8
`inline+concat`	20.6	19.1	31.9	33.5	23.6	20.6	21.8	22.6	21.7	22.8
Trained on ECB										
Baseline	16.8	52.2	21.1	24.6	**18.7**	20.9	17.7	19.7	17.2	19.8
`concat-diff`	19.6	**52.9**	21.5	25.6	18.3	**21.9**	18.5	20.7	18.1	**21.1**
`concat`	19.4	52.6	21.6	25.7	18.7	22.8	18.3	21.4	18.4	20.6
`inline`	19.1	52.2	21.3	25.4	18.1	20.3	18.3	20.4	17.2	19.3
`inline+concat-diff`	**20.6**	52.6	**21.8**	26.1	18.3	21.4	**19.0**	21.2	18.3	18.8
`inline+concat`	20.3	52.4	21.7	**26.2**	17.3	21.5	18.7	**21.4**	**18.5**	18.2
Trained on EMEA										
Baseline	64.7	18.2	15.9	19.2	12.2	28.2	14.4	17.8	12.9	15.7
`concat-diff`	65.1	18.7	17.2	21.1	13.9	28.1	15.3	**19.0**	14.8	17.1
`concat`	**65.2**	18.8	17.1	20.8	12.1	27.8	15.9	18.9	14.8	17.1
`inline`	64.9	18.2	16.6	19.5	**13.2**	28.3	15.0	17.6	13.5	15.6
`inline+concat-diff`	64.9	**19.0**	17.4	**21.4**	11.8	**28.4**	**16.4**	18.4	**15.8**	**17.6**
`inline+concat`	64.9	18.9	**17.4**	21.4	12.0	**28.4**	16.3	18.3	15.1	17.1

Table 4: BLEU scores of each domain-specific model on each of the test sets. The coloured cells indicate that the training and test data are from a similar domain. The highest BLEU score for each model on each test set is marked in bold.

	Real Definition	Fake definition
Source	Sie haben zur Befestigung ein 16mm Hülse als Anschluß, damit können Sie direkt an Ihr Fotostativ **<def>a photo tripod</def>**.	Sie haben zur Befestigung ein 16mm Hülse als Anschluß, damit können Sie direkt an Ihr Fotostativ **<def>green box</def>**.
ECB	You have a 16 mm sleeve for attaching it so you can attach it directly to your photo tripod.	You have a 16 mm sleeve for attaching it so you can attach it directly to your photo stative.
EMEA	You have a 16 mm needle attached to it so that you can directly attach it to your photogravure.	You have a 16 mm needle attached to it so that you can directly attach it to your photogravure.
GlobalVoices	They have a 16mm housing so you can hang it directly on your photo tripod.	They have a 16mm housing so you can hang directly on your photo stative.
Source	Immer neue Omikron-Fälle **<def>a variant of corona virus</def>** besorgen Politik und Wissenschaft in Großbritannien.	Immer neue Omikron-Fälle **<def>green box</def>** besorgen Politik und Wissenschaft in Großbritannien.
ECB	Policy and science in the UK are providing every new case of Omikron.	Each new case of Omikron provides policy and science in the UK.
EMEA	Manage new cases of Omicron in the UK, policy and science in the UK.	Manage new cases of Omicron in the context of policy and science in the UK.
GlobalVoices	New cases of Omicron are increasingly affecting Britain's politics and science.	New micron cases are increasingly creating a boost to Britain's politics and science.

Table 5: Examples of `inline` outputs created during our manual analysis of actual and fake annotations.

absolute scores. We train on each of the training sets in Table 3 and evaluate each one on all test sets.

5 Results

To test `inline`'s ability to transfer to new domains, we train one model per training dataset and evaluate on all test sets. We compare to `concat` approaches and to a baseline that does not use the lexicon, trained and evaluated in the same way. Given that `inline` only sees the lexicon words seen in the training data, we also test a hybrid approach involving training on the concatenation of both data sources and then fine-tuning using the inline approach. We compare a total of five models:

- `baseline` (no lexicon)
- `concat-diff`: concatenate lexicon and parallel data, with different prefixes
- `concat`: concatenate lexicon and parallel data
- `inline`: target lexicon entries are inserted inline into the source sentence
- `inline+concat-diff` and `inline+concat`: combinations of `inline` and either `concat-diff` or `concat`.

Results are shown in Table 4.[15] As expected, all baseline models perform well on data from the same

[15] Similar trends were seen using COMET (Rei et al., 2020) and

domain as the training data and struggle when tested on data from different domains. For example, the EMEA model has scores of 64.70 and 28.18 on the EMEA and Med20 test sets respectively, whereas it obtained less than 20 BLEU points on the other test sets. This supports the idea that NMT models are sensitive to out-of-domain data, as previously seen (Koehn and Knowles, 2017).

Compared to the baseline, both `concat` approaches improve the EMEA and ECB models' performance by at least 1 BLEU on a majority of the test sets from different domains. However, they do not provide any gains to the GlobalVoices model's performance on other domains. This may be because of the small size of the GlobalVoices training data (the bilingual lexicon contains 30k more examples and so possibly outweighs it). The `inline` model trained on GlobalVoices does not show improved performance on most of the test sets either. However, similar to the `concat` models' results, there was at least +0.5 BLEU when transferring from ECB→{EMEA,News18,News20,eComm22} and EMEA→{GV,News20,News22,Soc22}.

These results indicate that there is some evidence for cross-domain transfer for both approaches, which show small improvements for the ECB and EMEA models when evaluated on a different domain (although GlobalVoices models show little improvement, possibly due to the small dataset size). However, there is little improvement when these models are tested on the data from the same source as the training data (e.g. EMEA→EMEA and ECB→ECB). The hybrid approaches show some benefits over the individual methods in several cases especially for `inline+concat-diff`.

6 Going Further: When are Inline Definitions Used?

These results show that the inline approach leads to slight improvements in translation performance in some cases and does not improve in others. Examples 2-4 from the EMEA test sets (using the ECB-trained model) illustrate how attaching the candidates inline can sometimes be effectively used in the generated hypothesis and sometimes not. The models fail to use the annotations in Example 2, while they are partially and fully used in Examples 3 and 4 respectively.

(2) **Source:** transDeEn: - können Sie schwere *Migräne* <def>migraine</def> bekommen.
Target: - you may develop a severe migraine.
Baseline: - you can be vulnerable to severe crises.
`inline`: - you can become vulnerable to severe migration.

(3) **Source:** transDeEn: NovoMix 70 Penfill Patronen dürfen nicht wieder *aufgefüllt* <def>filled up, refilled, replenished</def> werden.
Target: Do not refill NovoMix 70 Penfill cartridges.
Baseline: Novo mix 70 penfill patrones must not be re-filled.
`inline`: Novo mix 70 penfills cannot be refilled.

(4) **Source:** transDeEn: Es enthält den *Wirkstoff* <def>active agent</def> Docetaxel.
Target: It contains the active substance docetaxel.
Baseline: contains Docetaxel.
`inline`: It contains the active agent Docetaxel.

We did some initial experimentation with the inline models by manually sampling examples from the test sets and creating hypothetical test examples (either with manually created correct translations or invented (incorrect) translations). A few such examples are shown in Table 5, whereby the fake candidate translations are simply composed of the word "green box". This preliminary analysis shows that rather than blindly copying, the models seem to make selective use of the definitions, which leads us to conduct a more systematic analysis.

6.1 Experimental Settings

We provide a more systematic analysis by creating artificial test cases, where we modify the inline translation candidates either by (i) replacing them with random translation candidates and (ii) prepending or appending the random candidates to the true ones. We show results for `inline` trained on ECB data and testing on EMEA, although we see similar results across the other models and test sets.

Rather than taking truly random contrastive translation candidates, we select random candidates amongst those whose headword matches the part of speech (POS) tag of the annotated source word.[16] To ensure the definitions are not too long, we only prepend/append alternative candidates containing a maximum of 4 tokens.

The four setups are illustrated in Examples 5-8:

(5) Original (green):
Source: transDeEn: Was Xagrid enthält Der *Wirkstoff*

will include these results in the appendix. We report BLEU instead of COMET since the conclusions are the same for the two metrics. COMET is better correlated with human judgments and is recommended by (Alam et al., 2021) for evaluation terminology translation, but BLEU is more tangible, so readers familiar with MT can get a better appreciation of absolute quality.

[16]In practice, we apply the POS tagger to the training data to determine the POS tag of potential headwords.

<def>active agent</def> ist Anagrelid.
Target: What Xagrid contains The active substance is anagrelide.

(6) Random replacement (underlined, red):
Source: transDeEn: Was Xagrid enthält Der *Wirkstoff* <def>economics</def> ist Anagrelid.

(7) Random prepended (underlined, red):
Source: transDeEn: Was Xagrid enthält Der *Wirkstoff* <def>veep, vice president, active agent</def> ist Anagrelid.

(8) Random appended (underlined, red):
Source: transDeEn: Was Xagrid enthält Der *Wirkstoff* <def>active agent, veep, vice president</def> ist Anagrelid.

In order to approximate whether the model is using the candidate translations in the inline annotations, for each annotated source word, we count the number of times the candidate annotation appears in the resulting translation outputs. We acknowledge the limitations of this approach: (i) we may get false positives when the candidate term appears elsewhere in the translation (and not as a translation of the annotated word), but these instances should be few given the rarity of the words in question, and (ii) as shown in Example 1, there are cases where the candidates do not appear in the reference at all. Nevertheless, this method gives us a way of getting a global picture of what is going on, particularly when it comes to copying behaviour. Since there can be multiple candidates, as well as multi-word candidates, we count the number of exact matches (the whole annotation appears) and partial matches, i.e. where one of the (comma-separated) candidates exists.[17]

6.2 Analysis Results

Do the models make use of the definitions? From our analysis using the manually and systematically created examples we found that these models make use of the definitions attached to unknown and rare words. However, we also found that the models use definitions that do not fit into the context of the input sentences rarely, at least far more frequently than for real definitions.

How often are the translation candidates used? Figure 1a shows how often the original candidate translations are used, either fully or partially. The full annotations appeared 563 times in the output, of which 222 were also in the baseline output. Importantly, a far higher number of candidates (341) only

[17] For partial matches, we remove stopwords such as *the* and *to* from definitions.

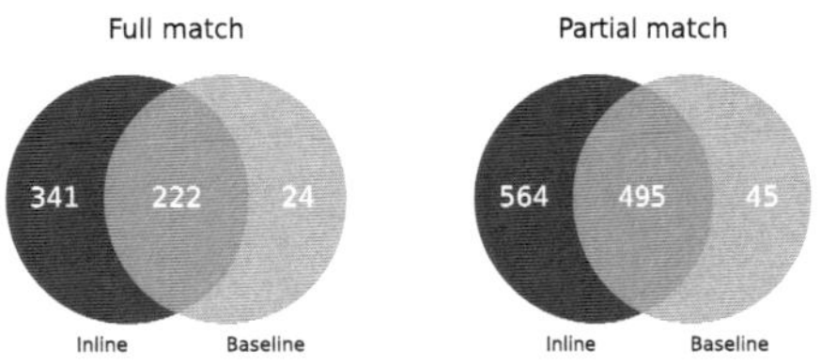

(a) Translation candidates from the lexicon

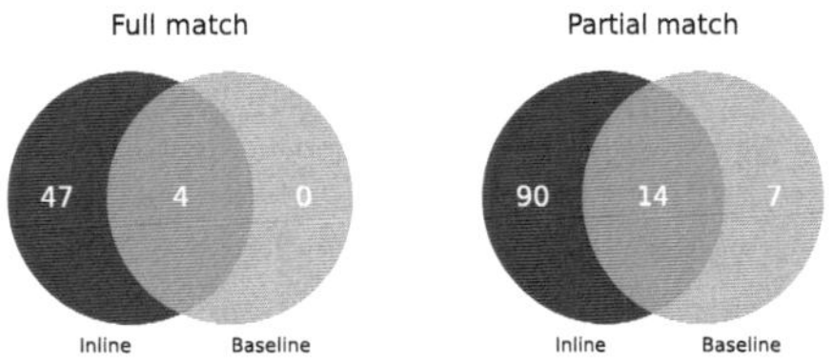

(b) Randomly selected translation candidates

Figure 1: Frequency of translation candidates used in the `inline` outputs compared to the baseline.

appeared in the `inline` outputs compared to the baseline ones (24), showing that `inline` is learning to copy the candidates. We see the same pattern for partial matches (one of the multiple candidates), again with the `inline` outputs containing far more candidate translations. This trend was consistent across the models and test sets that we analysed.

Figure 1b shows the number of candidates in the outputs when they are replaced by random (incorrect) annotations. The results indicate that the models rarely employ the incorrect definitions (i.e. they learn to discriminate between useful and irrelevant annotations). In fact, only 51 (for exact annotations) and 104 (for partial annotations) instances were detected in the `inline` translation outputs.

Can the model avoid distractor annotations? Instead of just replacing the annotation with a random replacement, we also analyse the setup where we combine the original annotations with the random ones (by prepending or appending). The results being very similar for the two cases, we only show results for the case of appending. Figure 2a shows the number of times the original annotations appear in the model outputs and 2b the number of times the distractor annotation appears. The pattern is the same as in Figure 1; the models rarely use the distractor annotations and although the number of true translation candidates decreases a little when distractors are used, the models is largely able to select and use the true annotations.

Evaluation in a higher-resource setting We also evaluate the methods in a higher-resource setting

Setup	OpenSubs	EMEA	ECB	GV	News18	News20	Med20	News22	eCom22	Soc22	Conv22
Trained on Multi-domain/high-resource											
Zero-shot	**33.6**	18.0	16.3	28.2	36.4	24.9	20.8	21.8	23.4	22.1	20.5
Baseline	32.6	50.1	**42.2**	32.2	38.2	**29.1**	31.4	**24.4**	24.9	**24.9**	**23.8**
`concat-diff`	32.4	50.2	42.1	32.2	**38.6**	29.0	31.1	24.3	24.8	24.7	23.6
`concat`	32.5	50.1	42.1	32.2	38.4	29.0	31.0	24.3	24.6	24.8	23.0
`inline`	32.6	**50.3**	42.1	**32.3**	38.4	28.6	**33.1**	24.3	**25.4**	**24.9**	23.4
`inline+concat-diff`	32.4	50.2	42.1	**32.3**	38.4	28.8	32.4	**24.4**	25.3	24.8	23.7
`inline+concat`	32.4	**50.3**	**42.2**	**32.3**	38.5	28.9	32.5	24.0	25.3	24.8	23.3

Table 6: BLEU scores of the general/multi domain model on each of the test sets. The highest BLEU score for each model on each test set is marked in bold.

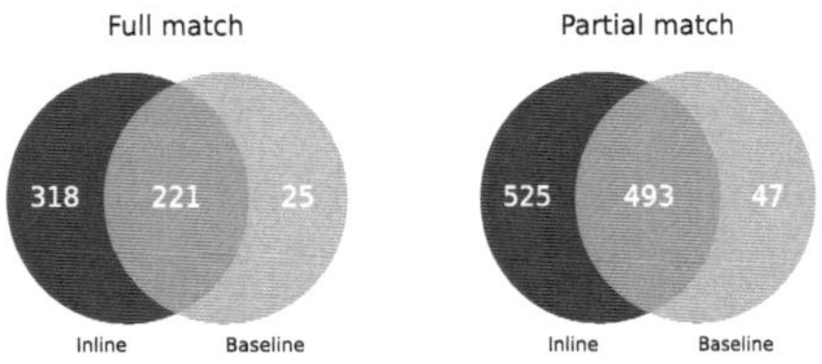

(a) Translation candidates from the lexicon

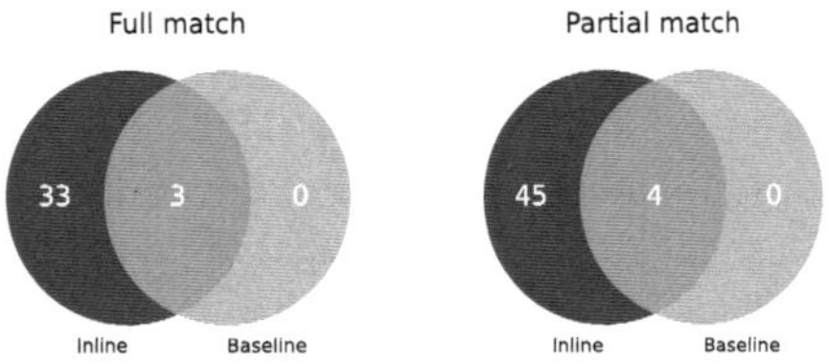

(b) Randomly selected translation candidates

Figure 2: Frequency of translation candidates used in the `inline` outputs (vs. baseline outputs) when appending random candidates.

with access to a wider vocabulary and from a multi-domain setting. Instead of just fine-tuning on the domain-specific training sets, we fine-tune mt5 in several steps: (i) firstly on data from OpenSubtitles2018[18] (Lison et al., 2018) for one epoch (due to its substantial size) and then (ii) on a combination of the EMEA, ECB, and GlobalVoices datasets and 250k randomly sampled parallel sentences from OpenSubtitles to avoid overfitting. We also use a larger lexicon; we extracted and cleaned a bilingual lexicon from Wiktionary[19] and merged it with Freedict.[20] For `inline`, words are considered unknown if they appear fewer than 20 times in the combined training data (from OpenSubtitles, EMEA, ECB, and GlobalVoices). Similar to the previous experiments, we created LSH using a threshold 0.6.

As previously, we report automatic scores (see Table 6) and our automatic analysis of matching words (see Figure 4). None of the methods outperform the baseline model. However the count statistics show that these models still use relevant entries and ignore irrelevant ones, but to a lesser extent than in the lower-resourced setting.

We also conducted a human evaluation involving two annotators with the aim of answering three questions: firstly, to confirm our automatic analysis, (i) which model output is better between the baseline and `inline`? and (ii) are the terms present in the source side of the `inline` model more present in the outputs than in the baseline? and finally, (iii) what sort of errors can we see? We focused on examples from the Med20 dataset where the `inline` appeared to exhibit better performance than the baseline. We selected all sentences with a single annotation, resulting in 81 distinct examples. We see (Figure 3) that a majority of translations were of the same quality, with a slight preference for `inline` (+4.32% over the baseline). We also observed a similar trend in how `inline` translations related to `inline` outputs compared to the baseline (despite the baseline not having access to them), suggesting that the information is rarely being used in this higher-resource setting, given the similarity in the behaviour of the two models.

Finally, we observed some limitations in the LSH method, whereby a large number of term translations were incorrect with respect to the annotated term ("Not related" category). This is likely to be exaggerated with respect to our main results using Freedict due to the lexicon being larger and less clean. This highlights an interesting point: the inaccuracy of LSH matching, which is likely to be a reason for the model learning to copy in some instances and not in others (i.e. the behaviour seen in our main results), is likely to lead to term translations not being used when the effect is too great. Neither baseline nor `inline` translations were per-

[18]`http://www.opensubtitles.org`

[19]Using the procedure described at `http://en.wiktionary.org/wiki/User:Matthias_Buchmeier`.

[20]We omitted Wiktionary in our main experiments due to its comparatively noisy nature compared to Freedict.

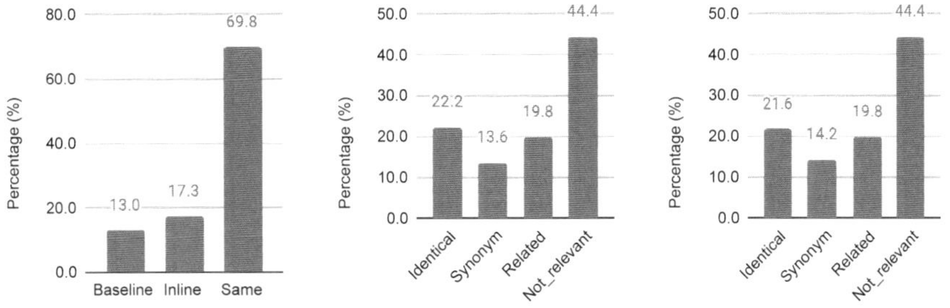

(a) Which system is better? (b) Relation (Baseline output) (c) Relation (`inline` output)

Figure 3: Human evaluation results of Med20 test set translations using the higher-resource multi-domain models. Figures 3b and 3c refer to the relation between annotated source words and their translations.

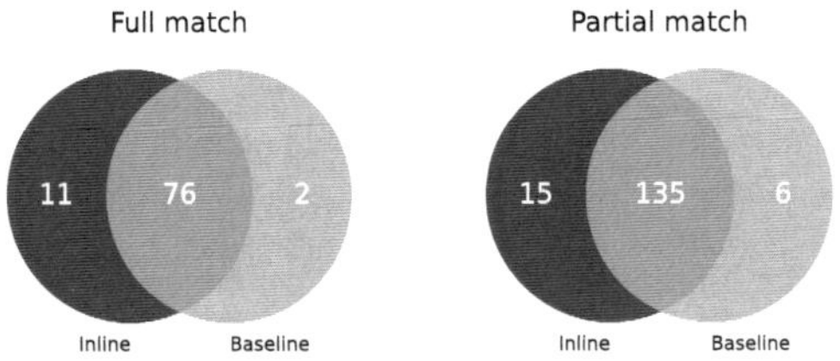

(a) Translation candidates from the lexicon

Figure 4: Frequency of translation candidates used in the `inline` outputs (vs. baseline outputs) in a multi-domain and high-resource setting.

fect, with many remaining term problems, so it appears that there is still research to be done on improving the approach.

7 Conclusions

Our study focuses on a simple method of incorporating lexical knowledge from bilingual lexicons into NMT models for cross-domain transfer: infixing translation candidates to rare terms within source sentences. We compare to using lexicon entries as additional parallel training data. We show that lexicons can sometimes help cross-domain transfer, but the gains seen (according to automatic metrics) are limited and appear to diminish in higher-resource scenarios. This is in contrast to its previous successful use in controlled language settings, showing that it is not such a promising approach in the general translation setting. Our analysis of the model outputs using distractor term translations showed that, despite the small difference in scores, the models make use of these definitions and they importantly can learn to ignore irrelevant definitions rather than blindly copying entries. However, the method is far from being as successful for this cross-domain setup as in the controlled language settings in which the method was developed, and experiments on a higher-resource language setting show that the approach does not have a huge effect to performance compared to a strong baseline.

Ethical Considerations and Limitations

There are several limitations of this work and directions for future research. Firstly, we focus on one particular language pair and leave testing in a multilingual setting to future work. In terms of the bilingual lexicons we used, we were limited to a lexicon containing fewer than 150,000 entries, along with some inherent noise in its contents. We hope that future research efforts will focus on expanding bilingual lexicon resources for a wider range of languages, particularly those with limited linguistic resources, and we see promise for studying these strategies in lower-resource scenarios. Also in this work, we associated unknown words with candidate translations using the previously proposed LSH method without any contextual information with the aim of seeing how this method could work in our domain transfer setting. We have shown that this method is insufficient and most likely led to an excess of noise in the annotations for the higher-resource scenario. In future work we could also focus on better methods for annotating the data.

Acknowledgements

Both authors' contributions were funded by R. Bawden's Emergence project, DadaNMT, funded by Sorbonne Université. R. Bawden was also funded by her chair position in the PRAIRIE institute funded by the French national agency ANR as part of the "Investissements d'avenir" programme under the reference ANR-19-P3IA-0001.

References

Akhbardeh, Farhad, Arkady Arkhangorodsky, Magdalena Biesialska, Ondřej Bojar, Rajen Chatterjee, Vishrav Chaudhary, Marta R. Costa-jussa, Cristina España-Bonet, Angela Fan, Christian Federmann, Markus Freitag, Yvette Graham, Roman Grundkiewicz, Barry Haddow, Leonie Harter, Kenneth Heafield, Christopher Homan, Matthias Huck, Kwabena Amponsah-Kaakyire, Jungo Kasai, Daniel Khashabi, Kevin Knight, Tom Kocmi, Philipp Koehn, Nicholas Lourie, Christof Monz, Makoto Morishita, Masaaki Nagata, Ajay Nagesh, Toshiaki Nakazawa, Matteo Negri, Santanu Pal, Allahsera Auguste Tapo, Marco Turchi, Valentin Vydrin, and Marcos Zampieri. 2021. Findings of the 2021 conference on machine translation (WMT21). In Barrault, Loic, Ondrej Bojar, Fethi Bougares, Rajen Chatterjee, Marta R. Costa-jussa, Christian Federmann, Mark Fishel, Alexander Fraser, Markus Freitag, Yvette Graham, Roman Grundkiewicz, Paco Guzman, Barry Haddow, Matthias Huck, Antonio Jimeno Yepes, Philipp Koehn, Tom Kocmi, Andre Martins, Makoto Morishita, and Christof Monz, editors, *Proceedings of the Sixth Conference on Machine Translation*, pages 1–88, Online, November. Association for Computational Linguistics.

Alam, Md Mahfuz Ibn, Ivana Kvapilíková, Antonios Anastasopoulos, Laurent Besacier, Georgiana Dinu, Marcello Federico, Matthias Gallé, Kweonwoo Jung, Philipp Koehn, and Vassilina Nikoulina. 2021. Findings of the WMT shared task on machine translation using terminologies. In Barrault, Loic, Ondrej Bojar, Fethi Bougares, Rajen Chatterjee, Marta R. Costa-jussa, Christian Federmann, Mark Fishel, Alexander Fraser, Markus Freitag, Yvette Graham, Roman Grundkiewicz, Paco Guzman, Barry Haddow, Matthias Huck, Antonio Jimeno Yepes, Philipp Koehn, Tom Kocmi, Andre Martins, Makoto Morishita, and Christof Monz, editors, *Proceedings of the Sixth Conference on Machine Translation*, pages 652–663, Online, November. Association for Computational Linguistics.

Arthaud, Farid, Rachel Bawden, and Alexandra Birch. 2021. Few-shot learning through contextual data augmentation. In Merlo, Paola, Jorg Tiedemann, and Reut Tsarfaty, editors, *Proceedings of the 16th Conference of the European Chapter of the Association for Computational Linguistics: Main Volume*, pages 1049–1062, Online, April. Association for Computational Linguistics.

Arthur, Philip, Graham Neubig, and Satoshi Nakamura. 2016. Incorporating discrete translation lexicons into neural machine translation. In Su, Jian, Kevin Duh, and Xavier Carreras, editors, *Proceedings of the 2016 Conference on Empirical Methods in Natural Language Processing*, pages 1557–1567, Austin, Texas, November. Association for Computational Linguistics.

Barrault, Loïc, Magdalena Biesialska, Ondřej Bojar, Marta R. Costa-jussà, Christian Federmann, Yvette Graham, Roman Grundkiewicz, Barry Haddow, Matthias Huck, Eric Joanis, Tom Kocmi, Philipp Koehn, Chi-kiu Lo, Nikola Ljubešić, Christof Monz, Makoto Morishita, Masaaki Nagata, Toshiaki Nakazawa, Santanu Pal, Matt Post, and Marcos Zampieri. 2020. Findings of the 2020 conference on machine translation (WMT20). In Barrault, Loïc, Ondřej Bojar, Fethi Bougares, Rajen Chatterjee, Marta R. Costa-jussà, Christian Federmann, Mark Fishel, Alexander Fraser, Yvette Graham, Paco Guzman, Barry Haddow, Matthias Huck, Antonio Jimeno Yepes, Philipp Koehn, André Martins, Makoto Morishita, Christof Monz, Masaaki Nagata, Toshiaki Nakazawa, and Matteo Negri, editors, *Proceedings of the Fifth Conference on Machine Translation*, pages 1–55, Online, November. Association for Computational Linguistics.

Bogoychev, Nikolay and Pinzhen Chen. 2021. The highs and lows of simple lexical domain adaptation approaches for neural machine translation. In Sedoc, João, Anna Rogers, Anna Rumshisky, and Shabnam Tafreshi, editors, *Proceedings of the Second Workshop on Insights from Negative Results in NLP*, pages 74–80, Online and Punta Cana, Dominican Republic, November. Association for Computational Linguistics.

Bosc, Tom and Pascal Vincent. 2018. Auto-encoding dictionary definitions into consistent word embeddings. In Riloff, Ellen, David Chiang, Julia Hockenmaier, and Jun'ichi Tsujii, editors, *Proceedings of the 2018 Conference on Empirical Methods in Natural Language Processing*, pages 1522–1532, Brussels, Belgium, October-November. Association for Computational Linguistics.

Caswell, Isaac, Ciprian Chelba, and David Grangier. 2019. Tagged back-translation. In Bojar, Ondřej, Rajen Chatterjee, Christian Federmann, Mark Fishel, Yvette Graham, Barry Haddow, Matthias Huck, Antonio Jimeno Yepes, Philipp Koehn, André Martins, Christof Monz, Matteo Negri, Aurélie Névéol, Mariana Neves, Matt Post, Marco Turchi, and Karin Verspoor, editors, *Proceedings of the Fourth Conference on Machine Translation (Volume 1: Research Papers)*, pages 53–63, Florence, Italy, August. Association for Computational Linguistics.

Clinchant, Stephane, Kweon Woo Jung, and Vassilina Nikoulina. 2019. On the use of BERT for neural machine translation. In Birch, Alexandra, Andrew Finch, Hiroaki Hayashi, Ioannis Konstas, Thang Luong, Graham Neubig, Yusuke Oda, and Katsuhito Sudoh, editors, *Proceedings of the 3rd Workshop on Neural Generation and Translation*, pages 108–117, Hong Kong, November. Association for Computational Linguistics.

Crego, Josep, Jungi Kim, Guillaume Klein, Anabel Rebollo, Kathy Yang, Jean Senellart, Egor Akhanov, Patrice Brunelle, Aurelien Coquard, Yongchao Deng, Satoshi Enoue, Chiyo Geiss, Joshua Johanson, Ardas Khalsa, Raoum Khiari, Byeongil Ko, Catherine Kobus, Jean Lorieux, Leidiana Martins, Dang-Chuan

Nguyen, Alexandra Priori, Thomas Riccardi, Natalia Segal, Christophe Servan, Cyril Tiquet, Bo Wang, Jin Yang, Dakun Zhang, Jing Zhou, and Peter Zoldan. 2016. Systran's pure neural machine translation systems.

Devlin, Jacob, Ming-Wei Chang, Kenton Lee, and Kristina Toutanova. 2019. BERT: Pre-training of deep bidirectional transformers for language understanding. In Burstein, Jill, Christy Doran, and Thamar Solorio, editors, *Proceedings of the 2019 Conference of the North American Chapter of the Association for Computational Linguistics: Human Language Technologies, Volume 1 (Long and Short Papers)*, pages 4171–4186, Minneapolis, Minnesota, June. Association for Computational Linguistics.

Dinu, Georgiana, Prashant Mathur, Marcello Federico, and Yaser Al-Onaizan. 2019. Training neural machine translation to apply terminology constraints. In Korhonen, Anna, David Traum, and Lluís Màrquez, editors, *Proceedings of the 57th Annual Meeting of the Association for Computational Linguistics*, pages 3063–3068, Florence, Italy, July. Association for Computational Linguistics.

Duan, Xiangyu, Baijun Ji, Hao Jia, Min Tan, Min Zhang, Boxing Chen, Weihua Luo, and Yue Zhang. 2020. Bilingual dictionary based neural machine translation without using parallel sentences. In Jurafsky, Dan, Joyce Chai, Natalie Schluter, and Joel Tetreault, editors, *Proceedings of the 58th Annual Meeting of the Association for Computational Linguistics*, pages 1570–1579, Online, July. Association for Computational Linguistics.

Feng, Yang, Shiyue Zhang, Andi Zhang, Dong Wang, and Andrew Abel. 2017. Memory-augmented neural machine translation. In Palmer, Martha, Rebecca Hwa, and Sebastian Riedel, editors, *Proceedings of the 2017 Conference on Empirical Methods in Natural Language Processing*, pages 1390–1399, Copenhagen, Denmark, September. Association for Computational Linguistics.

Goodfellow, Ian J., Mehdi Mirza, Da Xiao, Aaron Courville, and Yoshua Bengio. 2013. An empirical investigation of catastrophic forgetting in gradient-based neural networks.

Hasler, Eva, Adrià de Gispert, Gonzalo Iglesias, and Bill Byrne. 2018. Neural machine translation decoding with terminology constraints. In Walker, Marilyn, Heng Ji, and Amanda Stent, editors, *Proceedings of the 2018 Conference of the North American Chapter of the Association for Computational Linguistics: Human Language Technologies, Volume 2 (Short Papers)*, pages 506–512, New Orleans, Louisiana, June. Association for Computational Linguistics.

Hasler, Eva, Tobias Domhan, Jonay Trenous, Ke Tran, Bill Byrne, and Felix Hieber. 2021. Improving the quality trade-off for neural machine translation multi-domain adaptation. In Moens, Marie-Francine, Xuanjing Huang, Lucia Specia, and Scott Wen-tau Yih, editors, *Proceedings of the 2021 Conference on Empirical Methods in Natural Language Processing*, pages 8470–8477, Online and Punta Cana, Dominican Republic, November. Association for Computational Linguistics.

Hu, Junjie, Mengzhou Xia, Graham Neubig, and Jaime Carbonell. 2019. Domain adaptation of neural machine translation by lexicon induction. In Korhonen, Anna, David Traum, and Lluís Màrquez, editors, *Proceedings of the 57th Annual Meeting of the Association for Computational Linguistics*, pages 2989–3001, Florence, Italy, July. Association for Computational Linguistics.

Joulin, Armand, Edouard Grave, Piotr Bojanowski, Matthijs Douze, Hérve Jégou, and Tomas Mikolov. 2016. Fasttext.zip: Compressing text classification models. *arXiv preprint arXiv:1612.03651*.

Joulin, Armand, Edouard Grave, Piotr Bojanowski, and Tomas Mikolov. 2017. Bag of tricks for efficient text classification. In *Proceedings of the 15th Conference of the European Chapter of the Association for Computational Linguistics: Volume 2, Short Papers*, pages 427–431, Valencia, Spain, April. Association for Computational Linguistics.

Junczys-Dowmunt, Marcin and Roman Grundkiewicz. 2016. Log-linear combinations of monolingual and bilingual neural machine translation models for automatic post-editing. In Bojar, Ondřej, Christian Buck, Rajen Chatterjee, Christian Federmann, Liane Guillou, Barry Haddow, Matthias Huck, Antonio Jimeno Yepes, Aurélie Névéol, Mariana Neves, Pavel Pecina, Martin Popel, Philipp Koehn, Christof Monz, Matteo Negri, Matt Post, Lucia Specia, Karin Verspoor, Jörg Tiedemann, and Marco Turchi, editors, *Proceedings of the First Conference on Machine Translation: Volume 2, Shared Task Papers*, pages 751–758, Berlin, Germany, August. Association for Computational Linguistics.

Kobus, Catherine, Josep Crego, and Jean Senellart. 2017. Domain control for neural machine translation. In Mitkov, Ruslan and Galia Angelova, editors, *Proceedings of the International Conference Recent Advances in Natural Language Processing, RANLP 2017*, pages 372–378, Varna, Bulgaria, September. INCOMA Ltd.

Koehn, Philipp and Rebecca Knowles. 2017. Six challenges for neural machine translation. In Luong, Thang, Alexandra Birch, Graham Neubig, and Andrew Finch, editors, *Proceedings of the First Workshop on Neural Machine Translation*, pages 28–39, Vancouver, August. Association for Computational Linguistics.

Koehn, Philipp, Hieu Hoang, Alexandra Birch, Chris Callison-Burch, Marcello Federico, Nicola Bertoldi, Brooke Cowan, Wade Shen, Christine Moran, Richard Zens, Chris Dyer, Ondřej Bojar, Alexandra Constantin, and Evan Herbst. 2007. Moses: Open source toolkit for statistical machine translation. In

Ananiadou, Sophia, editor, *Proceedings of the 45th Annual Meeting of the Association for Computational Linguistics Companion Volume Proceedings of the Demo and Poster Sessions*, pages 177–180, Prague, Czech Republic, June. Association for Computational Linguistics.

Lample, Guillaume and Alexis Conneau. 2019. Cross-lingual language model pretraining. In *Proceedings of the 33rd Conference on Neural Information Processing Systems (NeurIPS 2019)*, Vancouver, Canada, January.

Lison, Pierre, Jörg Tiedemann, and Milen Kouylekov. 2018. OpenSubtitles2018: Statistical rescoring of sentence alignments in large, noisy parallel corpora. In Calzolari, Nicoletta, Khalid Choukri, Christopher Cieri, Thierry Declerck, Sara Goggi, Koiti Hasida, Hitoshi Isahara, Bente Maegaard, Joseph Mariani, Hélène Mazo, Asuncion Moreno, Jan Odijk, Stelios Piperidis, and Takenobu Tokunaga, editors, *Proceedings of the Eleventh International Conference on Language Resources and Evaluation (LREC 2018)*, Miyazaki, Japan, May. European Language Resources Association (ELRA).

Liu, Yinhan, Jiatao Gu, Naman Goyal, Xian Li, Sergey Edunov, Marjan Ghazvininejad, Mike Lewis, and Luke Zettlemoyer. 2020. Multilingual denoising pre-training for neural machine translation. *Transactions of the Association for Computational Linguistics*, 8:726–742.

Michon, Elise, Josep Crego, and Jean Senellart. 2020. Integrating domain terminology into neural machine translation. In Scott, Donia, Nuria Bel, and Chengqing Zong, editors, *Proceedings of the 28th International Conference on Computational Linguistics*, pages 3925–3937, Barcelona, Spain (Online), December. International Committee on Computational Linguistics.

Niehues, Jan. 2021. Continuous learning in neural machine translation using bilingual dictionaries. In Merlo, Paola, Jorg Tiedemann, and Reut Tsarfaty, editors, *Proceedings of the 16th Conference of the European Chapter of the Association for Computational Linguistics: Main Volume*, pages 830–840, Online, April. Association for Computational Linguistics.

Papineni, Kishore, Salim Roukos, Todd Ward, and Wei-Jing Zhu. 2002. Bleu: a method for automatic evaluation of machine translation. In Isabelle, Pierre, Eugene Charniak, and Dekang Lin, editors, *Proceedings of the 40th Annual Meeting of the Association for Computational Linguistics*, pages 311–318, Philadelphia, Pennsylvania, USA, July. Association for Computational Linguistics.

Pham, Ngoc-Quan, Jan Niehues, and Alexander Waibel. 2018. Towards one-shot learning for rare-word translation with external experts. In Birch, Alexandra, Andrew Finch, Thang Luong, Graham Neubig, and Yusuke Oda, editors, *Proceedings of the 2nd Workshop on Neural Machine Translation and Generation*, pages 100–109, Melbourne, Australia, July. Association for Computational Linguistics.

Pham, Minhquang, Josep Maria Crego, and François Yvon. 2021. Revisiting multi-domain machine translation. *Transactions of the Association for Computational Linguistics*, 9:17–35.

Post, Matt. 2018. A call for clarity in reporting BLEU scores. In Bojar, Ondřej, Rajen Chatterjee, Christian Federmann, Mark Fishel, Yvette Graham, Barry Haddow, Matthias Huck, Antonio Jimeno Yepes, Philipp Koehn, Christof Monz, Matteo Negri, Aurélie Névéol, Mariana Neves, Matt Post, Lucia Specia, Marco Turchi, and Karin Verspoor, editors, *Proceedings of the Third Conference on Machine Translation: Research Papers*, pages 186–191, Brussels, Belgium, October. Association for Computational Linguistics.

Ramírez-Sánchez, Gema, Jaume Zaragoza-Bernabeu, Marta Bañón, and Sergio Ortiz Rojas. 2020. Bifixer and bicleaner: two open-source tools to clean your parallel data. In Martins, André, Helena Moniz, Sara Fumega, Bruno Martins, Fernando Batista, Luisa Coheur, Carla Parra, Isabel Trancoso, Marco Turchi, Arianna Bisazza, Joss Moorkens, Ana Guerberof, Mary Nurminen, Lena Marg, and Mikel L. Forcada, editors, *Proceedings of the 22nd Annual Conference of the European Association for Machine Translation*, pages 291–298, Lisboa, Portugal, November. European Association for Machine Translation.

Rei, Ricardo, Craig Stewart, Ana C Farinha, and Alon Lavie. 2020. COMET: A neural framework for MT evaluation. In Webber, Bonnie, Trevor Cohn, Yulan He, and Yang Liu, editors, *Proceedings of the 2020 Conference on Empirical Methods in Natural Language Processing (EMNLP)*, pages 2685–2702, Online, November. Association for Computational Linguistics.

Sánchez-Cartagena, Víctor M., Marta Bañón, Sergio Ortiz-Rojas, and Gema Ramírez. 2018. Prompsit's submission to WMT 2018 parallel corpus filtering shared task. In Bojar, Ondřej, Rajen Chatterjee, Christian Federmann, Mark Fishel, Yvette Graham, Barry Haddow, Matthias Huck, Antonio Jimeno Yepes, Philipp Koehn, Christof Monz, Matteo Negri, Aurélie Névéol, Mariana Neves, Matt Post, Lucia Specia, Marco Turchi, and Karin Verspoor, editors, *Proceedings of the Third Conference on Machine Translation: Shared Task Papers*, pages 955–962, Belgium, Brussels, October. Association for Computational Linguistics.

Saunders, Danielle. 2021. Domain adaptation and multi-domain adaptation for neural machine translation: A survey. *CoRR*, abs/2104.06951.

Sennrich, Rico, Barry Haddow, and Alexandra Birch. 2016. Controlling politeness in neural machine translation via side constraints. In Knight, Kevin, Ani Nenkova, and Owen Rambow, editors, *Proceedings of the 2016 Conference of the North American Chapter of the Association for Computational Linguistics:*

Human Language Technologies, pages 35–40, San Diego, California, June. Association for Computational Linguistics.

Shi, Weijia, Muhao Chen, Yingtao Tian, and Kai-Wei Chang. 2019. Learning bilingual word embeddings using lexical definitions. In Augenstein, Isabelle, Spandana Gella, Sebastian Ruder, Katharina Kann, Burcu Can, Johannes Welbl, Alexis Conneau, Xiang Ren, and Marek Rei, editors, *Proceedings of the 4th Workshop on Representation Learning for NLP (RepL4NLP-2019)*, pages 142–147, Florence, Italy, August. Association for Computational Linguistics.

Song, Kai, Yue Zhang, Heng Yu, Weihua Luo, Kun Wang, and Min Zhang. 2019. Code-switching for enhancing NMT with pre-specified translation. In Burstein, Jill, Christy Doran, and Thamar Solorio, editors, *Proceedings of the 2019 Conference of the North American Chapter of the Association for Computational Linguistics: Human Language Technologies, Volume 1 (Long and Short Papers)*, pages 449–459, Minneapolis, Minnesota, June. Association for Computational Linguistics.

Tan, Liling, Josef van Genabith, and Francis Bond. 2015. Passive and pervasive use of bilingual dictionary in statistical machine translation. In Babych, Bogdan, Kurt Eberle, Patrik Lambert, Reinhard Rapp, Rafael E. Banchs, and Marta R. Costa-jussà, editors, *Proceedings of the Fourth Workshop on Hybrid Approaches to Translation (HyTra)*, pages 30–34, Beijing, July. Association for Computational Linguistics.

Tiedemann, Jörg. 2012. Parallel data, tools and interfaces in OPUS. In Calzolari, Nicoletta, Khalid Choukri, Thierry Declerck, Mehmet Uğur Doğan, Bente Maegaard, Joseph Mariani, Asuncion Moreno, Jan Odijk, and Stelios Piperidis, editors, *Proceedings of the Eighth International Conference on Language Resources and Evaluation (LREC'12)*, pages 2214–2218, Istanbul, Turkey, May. European Language Resources Association (ELRA).

Verma, Neha, Kenton Murray, and Kevin Duh. 2022. Strategies for adapting multilingual pre-training for domain-specific machine translation. In Duh, Kevin and Francisco Guzmán, editors, *Proceedings of the 15th biennial conference of the Association for Machine Translation in the Americas (Volume 1: Research Track)*, pages 31–44, Orlando, USA, September. Association for Machine Translation in the Americas.

Vu, Thuy-Trang, Xuanli He, Dinh Phung, and Gholamreza Haffari. 2021. Generalised unsupervised domain adaptation of neural machine translation with cross-lingual data selection. In Moens, Marie-Francine, Xuanjing Huang, Lucia Specia, and Scott Wen-tau Yih, editors, *Proceedings of the 2021 Conference on Empirical Methods in Natural Language Processing*, pages 3335–3346, Online and Punta Cana, Dominican Republic, November. Association for Computational Linguistics.

Wolf, Thomas, Lysandre Debut, Victor Sanh, Julien Chaumond, Clement Delangue, Anthony Moi, Pierric Cistac, Tim Rault, Remi Louf, Morgan Funtowicz, Joe Davison, Sam Shleifer, Patrick von Platen, Clara Ma, Yacine Jernite, Julien Plu, Canwen Xu, Teven Le Scao, Sylvain Gugger, Mariama Drame, Quentin Lhoest, and Alexander Rush. 2020. Transformers: State-of-the-art natural language processing. In Liu, Qun and David Schlangen, editors, *Proceedings of the 2020 Conference on Empirical Methods in Natural Language Processing: System Demonstrations*, pages 38–45, Online, October. Association for Computational Linguistics.

Xu, Jitao and François Yvon. 2021. Can you traducir this? machine translation for code-switched input. In Solorio, Thamar, Shuguang Chen, Alan W. Black, Mona Diab, Sunayana Sitaram, Victor Soto, Emre Yilmaz, and Anirudh Srinivasan, editors, *Proceedings of the Fifth Workshop on Computational Approaches to Linguistic Code-Switching*, pages 84–94, Online, June. Association for Computational Linguistics.

Xue, Linting, Noah Constant, Adam Roberts, Mihir Kale, Rami Al-Rfou, Aditya Siddhant, Aditya Barua, and Colin Raffel. 2021. mT5: A massively multilingual pre-trained text-to-text transformer. In Toutanova, Kristina, Anna Rumshisky, Luke Zettlemoyer, Dilek Hakkani-Tur, Iz Beltagy, Steven Bethard, Ryan Cotterell, Tanmoy Chakraborty, and Yichao Zhou, editors, *Proceedings of the 2021 Conference of the North American Chapter of the Association for Computational Linguistics: Human Language Technologies*, pages 483–498, Online, June. Association for Computational Linguistics.

Zhong, Xing Jie and David Chiang. 2020. Look it up: Bilingual dictionaries improve neural machine translation.

Setup	EMEA	ECB	GV	News18	News20	Med20	News22	eCom22	Soc22	Conv22
Trained on Globalvoices										
Baseline	0.756	0.759	0.846	0.818	0.778	0.772	0.781	0.771	0.778	0.801
`concat-diff`	0.758	0.757	0.848	0.819	0.777	0.776	0.778	0.775	0.776	0.801
`concat`	0.756	0.758	0.846	0.819	0.776	0.764	0.778	0.773	0.776	0.799
`inline`	0.761	0.761	0.848	0.821	0.784	0.781	0.781	0.774	0.782	0.797
`inline+concat-diff`	0.760	0.759	0.847	0.820	0.779	0.781	0.779	0.772	0.775	0.791
`inline+concat`	0.759	0.760	0.847	0.820	0.777	0.760	0.777	0.775	0.774	0.795
Trained on ECB										
Baseline	0.709	0.843	0.772	0.759	0.727	0.750	0.727	0.745	0.711	0.755
`concat-diff`	0.733	0.844	0.782	0.774	0.730	0.776	0.741	0.762	0.731	0.765
`concat`	0.732	0.843	0.785	0.775	0.737	0.773	0.739	0.762	0.731	0.761
`inline`	0.721	0.843	0.778	0.769	0.729	0.750	0.732	0.749	0.716	0.755
`inline+concat-diff`	0.738	0.843	0.786	0.780	0.734	0.766	0.744	0.759	0.733	0.756
`inline+concat`	0.739	0.843	0.788	0.780	0.733	0.771	0.747	0.757	0.735	0.764
Trained on EMEA										
Baseline	0.877	0.717	0.696	0.687	0.636	0.774	0.658	0.726	0.649	0.671
`concat-diff`	0.878	0.730	0.722	0.718	0.656	0.775	0.688	0.737	0.684	0.714
`concat`	0.878	0.729	0.724	0.716	0.653	0.775	0.687	0.741	0.685	0.715
`inline`	0.878	0.721	0.712	0.702	0.651	0.793	0.673	0.729	0.665	0.681
`inline+concat-diff`	0.878	0.734	0.733	0.727	0.659	0.777	0.696	0.743	0.695	0.721
`inline+concat`	0.878	0.730	0.735	0.727	0.659	0.781	0.699	0.747	0.696	0.724

Table 7: COMET scores of each domain-specific model on each of the test sets. The coloured cells indicate that the training and test data are from a similar domain.

A COMET scores for main results

Table 7 shows results using the COMET metric (Using the default model `Unbabel/wmt22-comet-da`.) (Rei et al., 2020) for the main results shown in Table 4. The trends we see are the same between the BLEU and COMET scores.

Adding soft terminology constraints to pre-trained generic MT models by means of continued training

Tommi Nieminen
University of Helsinki, Finland
tommi.nieminen@helsinki.fi

Abstract

This article describes an efficient method of adding terminology support to existing machine translation models. The training of the pre-trained models is continued with parallel data where strings identified as terms in the source language data have been annotated with the lemmas of the corresponding target terms. Evaluation using standard test sets and methods confirms that continued training from generic base models can produce term models that are competitive with models specifically trained as term models.

1 Introduction

One of the major challenges of using machine translation (MT) to enhance the productivity of human translators in professional translation is enforcing the use of correct terminology in MT output. In general, a translator is expected to adhere either to standard domain-specific terminology, or to a client-specific terminology, which can be provided as a dedicated terminology database (usually referred to as a *termbase*) or implicitly in the form of a translation memory. In the professional translation setting, when the output of a MT system diverges from the specified terminology, a translator needs to correct the output manually, significantly reducing the utility of MT. It is therefore important that a translator has the capability of influencing the terminological choices that the MT system makes by providing terminology to the system.

In this article, we introduce a method of adding support for enforcing user-provided terminology into existing MT models. The method is based on continued training of the model using data annotated with terminology information.

2 Related work

2.1 Constraining terminology in neural machine translation

The majority of methods of constraining an neural machine translation (NMT) model to use user-provided terminology in translations belong to four distinct categories.

Pass-through placeholders

Source terms in the source sentence are replaced by placeholders, and the NMT model reproduces the placeholders in the translation (Michon et al., 2020). The reproduced placeholders in the translation are then replaced by the target terms corresponding to the source terms that the placeholder had originally replaced. This approach requires that the model is trained with data that has been augmented with sentence pairs containing aligned placeholders on source and target sides. Using pass-through placeholders usually ensures that the target terms are generated in correct positions, but the information contained in the source term is lost and cannot be utilized by the model when generating the translation, which can lead to translation errors. It is also difficult to generate the correct morphological features for the target terms, especially for morphologically complex languages.

Constrained decoding

In constrained decoding, the search algorithm of the MT system is modified to ensure that target terms are generated for each source term identified in the source sentence. For instance, Hokamp and Liu (2017) introduce a variant of beam search

Proceedings of the First International Workshop on Knowledge-Enhanced Machine Translation, pages 21–33
June 27, 2024 ©2024 European Association for Machine Translation

called Grid Beam Search, which only produces hypotheses that contain the required target terms. The benefit of constrained decoding is that it can be used as an add-on component to any MT model. However, most constrained decoding implementations are much slower than normal beam search, and they may cause translation quality issues, as the required target terms will be used even in inappropriate contexts.

Adding target terms as soft constraints

The pass-through placeholder and constrained decoding methods treat terms as unconditional: they should always be included in the generated translation. In those methods, terms can therefore be referred to as hard constraints on the MT output.

It is also possible to add terms as soft constraints, which the MT model can override. The most common method of implementing terminology as soft constraints is to annotate the source data with terminology information. These annotations can be added in different ways. For instance, in the first published work on soft terminology constraints (Dinu et al., 2019), two methods were tested: the target term was either appended after the corresponding source term or the target term replaced the source term. Factors were used to signal that the target terms were to be processed differently from normal source tokens. Like the pass-through placeholder method, the soft constraint method requires that training data of the model is augmented, in this case with sentence pairs, where the source sentence has been annotated with target term information that also occurs in the target sentence. This causes the model to associate a target term in the source sentence with having the same target term in the target sentence.

The annotation-based soft constraint method seems to currently be the most popular and widely used method of enforcing user-provided terminology, and it has also been most successful and common in recent terminology MT shared tasks (Alam et al., 2021b; Semenov et al., 2023).

Using large language models

Large language models (LLMs) provide another way to apply terminology as soft constraints. With LLMs, the use of user-provided terminology can be enforced in several ways. Moslem et al. (2023a) implement constrained terminology in LLM translation by adding terminology translations to the prompts they use to elicit translations from the `GPT-3.5 text-davinci-003` model. Bogoychev and Chen (2023) use the `gpt-3.5-turbo-0613` model to correct terminology in an unconstrained LLM translation by providing a refined prompt containing the required terminology changes. LLMs can also be used to post-edit the terminology in translations generated by conventional NMT systems (Moslem et al., 2023b).

2.2 Continued training

In continued training (also called fine-tuning), the training of a pre-trained NMT model is continued with a training set that is usually either a distinct subset of the original training data of the pre-trained model or a new data set which was not included in the original training data, at least not in its entirety. The most common use case for continued training is domain adaptation, for instance adapting a pre-trained generic NMT model to speech translation using speech data (Luong and Manning, 2015). Continued training has also been used for adding new language pairs to a multilingual NMT model (Neubig and Hu, 2018), and to alleviate the effects of large amounts of back-translated data on translation quality by continuing training with only genuine parallel data (Bawden et al., 2019).

Continued training is widely used in NMT research and industry, and its effectiveness has been demonstrated with manual evaluation (Dogru and Moorkens, 2024). However, continued training always entails a risk of catastrophic forgetting (Mccloskey and Cohen, 1989), where the model partially or completely loses the ability to translate source text that is not present in the training set used for the continued training.

3 Model training

We generate models with terminology support (term models) for multiple language pairs by continuing the training of generic base models with data annotated with terminology information.

Pre-trained models published as part of the Tatoeba-Challenge (Tiedemann, 2020)[1] project are used as the base models for the continued training. Tatoeba-Challenge project includes MT models for hundreds of language pairs, and for many language pairs there are multiple models available. According to automatic evaluations performed on

[1] https://github.com/Helsinki-NLP/Tatoeba-Challenge

the Tatoeba-Challenge models, the models with the best performance are based on the *transformer-big* architecture. However, as we intend to deploy these terminology models for low-latency CPU inference on desktop computers, we use the *transformer-base* models, which generate translations much quicker.

	Base model
en-bg	opus+bt-2021-04-13
en-da	opus+bt-2021-04-13
en-de	opus+bt-2021-04-13
en-es	opus+bt-2021-04-10
en-et	opus-2019-12-18
en-fi	opusTCv20210807+bt-2021-09-01
en-fr	opus-2021-02-22
en-it	opus+bt-2021-04-14
en-lt	opus+bt-2021-04-14
en-nl	opus+bt-2021-04-14
en-sv	opus+bt-2021-04-14
fi-en	opusTCv20210807+bt-2021-08-25

Table 1: Models that were used as base models for term fine-tuning (all are different bilingual models).

For the experiments, we selected a subset of language pairs for which base models of reasonable quality (according to the published automatic metrics[2]) were available. The selection includes 12 medium- and high-resource translation directions between different pairs of European languages. For some language pairs, such as English to Estonian, *transformer-base* models are not available among Tatoeba-Challenge models, and models from the OPUS-MT model collection (Tiedemann and Thottingal, 2020) are used instead. All models have been trained on data that has been segmented with `SentencePiece` (Kudo and Richardson, 2018) (see table 1 for the model names).

The continued training is performed with `MarianNMT` (Junczys-Dowmunt et al., 2018) using the default settings (v1.11.13). While adjusting hyperparameters, such as learning rate, might make the continued training more efficient, the initial automatic metric results indicated that the default settings were sufficient for the task, so we decided not to experiment with any hyperparameter adjustments. The duration of continued training was one epoch.

[2]https://opus.nlpl.eu/dashboard/

3.1 Data

The training of each model is continued with a subset of the Tatoeba-Challenge data set *v2023-09-26* for the language pair in question. Tatoeba-Challenge data sets contain most of the data available in the OPUS corpus collection (Tiedemann, 2009). The base models were originally trained with an earlier version of the Tatoeba-Challenge data set, so the original training data and the data for continued training overlap significantly. Since the data sets contain large proportions of crawled data, which often has quality issues (Kreutzer et al., 2022), Bicleaner-AI (Zaragoza-Bernabeu et al., 2022) scores (model version 2.0) are used to extract the best quality parallel sentence pairs to be used as the continued training set. Ten million best-scoring sentence pairs are extracted as fine-tuning data for each language pair.

3.2 Training pipeline

A modified version of Mozilla's *firefox-translations-training*[3] pipeline was used to train the models. This pipeline, which is based on the Snakemake workflow management system (Mölder et al., 2021), can perform all the steps required for building NMT models, such as loading, pre-processing, cleaning and filtering the training data, and training and evaluating the NMT models. For the work described in this article, terminology annotation and evaluation components were added to the pipeline. The code for the modified pipeline is available on GitHub.[4]

3.3 Terminology annotation

As mentioned, training data for soft constraint terminology training needs to be annotated with terminology information. Two different methods are commonly used for generating such annotated training data:

1. **Annotating a corpus using a termbase** (e.g. Dinu et al. (2019)): Given a termbase, such as IATE,[5] and a parallel corpus, search the parallel corpus for sentence pairs where the source sentence contains source terms from the termbase. For those sentence pairs with source terms, check for each source term whether the corresponding target term also

[3]https://github.com/mozilla/firefox-translations-training
[4]https://github.com/Helsinki-NLP/OpusDistillery/tree/eamt_opuscat_terms
[5]https://iate.europa.eu/home

occurs in the target sentence. Then annotate those source terms that have corresponding target terms with terminology information.

2. **Annotating a corpus using aligned pseudo-terms** (e.g. Bergmanis and Pinnis (2021)): Given a parallel corpus, align source and target tokens with an alignment tool such as `FastAlign` (Dyer et al., 2013). Then select aligned subsets of tokens and use them as pseudo-terms.

There are benefits and disadvantages to both of these methods: using a termbase ensures that the annotated terms are reasonable, but it also restricts the annotations to the subject matter of the database making them uniform, and unless the database is very large, there may not be enough term matches found in the parallel data to generate an annotated training set that is large enough. On the other hand, pseudo-terms may not bear much resemblance to actual terminology, unless their generation is restricted in some way. One major benefit of the pseudo-term approach is that it is language-independent, while the database approach is only usable for language pairs for which suitable termbases exist.

We use the aligned pseudo-term approach for reasons of simplicity. The pseudo-term generation is restricted to aligned noun and verb phrase chunks, as real-world terminology generally also consists of noun and verb phrases. The process for generating the annotated training data from parallel data is the following:

1. **Parse data to identify POS and dependencies:** Generate the parts-of-speech (POS) and dependency relations of source and target sentence tokens using `Stanza` (Qi et al., 2020).

2. **Create noun and verb chunks:** Identify noun and verb phrase chunks in the source and target sentences based on the POS and dependency information.

3. **Token alignment:** Align parallel corpus on token-level with FastAlign, using the *grow-diag-final-and* heuristic.

4. **Chunk alignment:** Use alignment information from step 3 to identify source noun chunks that are aligned to target noun chunks and source verb chunks that are aligned to target verb chunks.

5. **Appending target chunk lemmas to source chunks:** Append lemma forms of target chunks after the corresponding source chunks in the source sentence.

Our pseudo-term generation method is very similar to that used in (Bergmanis and Pinnis, 2021). The difference is that we align chunks instead of words, and the alignment is performed on the subword units of the sentences instead of the lemma forms of words in the sentence.

The parallel data is annotated with the pseudo-terms by appending the target term after the corresponding source term in the source sentence. The term annotation is indicated by using three indicator tags: one before the source term, one between the source term and the target term, and one after the target term. See table 2 for an example of the annotation scheme.

The annotation scheme is similar to the *append* method used in (Dinu et al., 2019). The main difference is that like Ailem et al. (2021) we use tags and not factors to indicate target terms. Lemma forms of target terms are used in the source sentence in order to make the model associate a lemma form in the source sentence with an inflected form in the target sentence, which is the behaviour that the model should ideally adapt during the training.

Any number of terms can occur in a source sentence, so the training data needs to contain source sentences with varying amounts of annotated terms. Our annotation script keeps a running count of the number of sentences with *n* terms that have been annotated, and ensures that there is variability in the amounts of terms in the training data sentence pairs. The amount of sentence pairs per term count approximates a geometric series, where the amount of sentence pairs is halved for each term. The ratio is chosen on the assumption that only a few terms will occur in most sentences, although in actual production cases the frequency of terms will probably vary greatly by domain and the scale and level of detail of the terminology database that is used.

For some sentence pairs in the training corpus, no aligned term chunks are found using the above method, so for each language pair there is a varying amount of sentence pairs without term annota-

Source	`British Library releases a million images on Flickr`
Annotated source	`British Library <term_start> releases <term_end> veröffentlichen <trans_end> a million <term_start> images </term_end> Bild <trans_end> on Flickr`

Table 2: Example of the annotation method scheme used in the experiments (note in the actual training data the sentences are split into sub-word units, here they appear unsegmented for clarity)

tions. To see the effect of having a mix of annotated and unannotated sentence pairs in the training corpus, two models are trained for each language pair: one with both unannotated and annotated sentence pairs, and one with only annotated sentence pairs (referred to as the *only-terms* model in the tables). See table 3 for amounts of sentences annotated with terms for each language pair.

	Annotated sentences
en-bg	7,604,181
en-da	7,441,517
en-de	6,092,623
en-es	5,782,967
en-et	7,226,641
en-fi	6,706,819
en-fr	4,599,385
en-it	3,143,592
en-lt	7,495,889
en-nl	7,358,655
en-sv	7,330,407
fi-en	6,510,906

Table 3: The amounts of sentences annotated with terms for each language pair. Annotated sentences contain 1.99 terms on average. *only-terms* models are trained with this data only, while *term* models are trained with the whole 10 million sentence pair training set, including sentence pairs without terms.

3.4 Vocabulary adaptation

The vocabularies of the base Tatoeba-Challenge models contain only symbols that have occurred in the original training corpus, i.e. the Tatoeba-Challenge data set segmented with SentencePiece. There are no spare symbols that can be used as terminology tags, so naturally occurring symbols have to be repurposed to act as the terminology tags. We use an automatic method to choose three uncommon vocabulary units to act as the terminology tags. As the symbols chosen as the terminology tags do not occur in the filtered training data (they are extremely rarely occurring tokens, such as characters from non-Latin scripts), re-purposing them should have no effect on translation quality.

4 Evaluation

There are three important aspects to the evaluation of NMT models with terminology support:

1. **Overall translation quality without terminology**: how well the model translates source sentences with no terms present.
2. **Terminological accuracy**: how many of the source terms have a corresponding target term present in the translation.
3. **Overall translation quality with terminology**: if the source sentence is annotated with terms, how well does the model translate the sentence (regardless of how many terms it gets correct).

Ideally, a terminology model translates terms accurately, while maintaining an overall translation quality level comparable to the base model, both when translating sentences with terms or without them. This kind of model can be used independently, with no supplementary models.

Minimally, a terminology translation model has to have a reasonable level of term accuracy without causing the overall translation quality of sentences with terminology to degrade too much. A term model with this kind of minimal performance can still be useful, as long as it is used together with a generic back-off model that translates sentences without terms.

4.1 Overall translation performance without terminology

The purpose of evaluating translation performance without terminology is to see if catastrophic forgetting occurs, i.e whether the continued training significantly degrades the term model's performance in general translation.

Metrics

Terminology models are compared against the base models using two automatic evaluation metrics. BLEU scores are generated using `sacrebleu` (Post, 2018), and additionally

COMET (Rei et al., 2020) scores are generated with the `wmt22-comet-da` model.

Data for evaluating translation performance without terms

For each language pair, a maximum of four test sets are downloaded using `sacrebleu` and `mtdata` (Gowda et al., 2021) tools. For most language pairs, WMT test sets from different years are used. If no WMT test sets are available for a language pair (such as English to Swedish), the FLORES test set (Goyal et al., 2021) is used instead. The test sets were compared with the fine-tuning sets to verify that there was no overlap that could affect the results.

The results of evaluation without terminology are listed in table 4.

4.2 Terminological accuracy

Term models are assessed on how well they reproduce the specified terminology in their outputs. The evaluation is primarily performed with the methods outlined in (Alam et al., 2021a), using the `terminology_evaluation` [6] script provided by the authors. As the script assumes tokenized and truecased input, we use a modified script that tokenizes and truecases the SentencePiece output from the models using Stanza. Due to this and other changes, the modified script is made separately available. [7]

The main evaluation metric included in the script is *Exact-Match Accuracy*, which scores a translation based on how many of the required target terms it contains. Despite the name, the metric also accepts inflected forms of the target terms in addition to exact matches.

The principal difficulty in judging the terminological correctness of a translation is that while it is simple to check if a translation contains the lemma or inflected forms of required target terms, it is not easy to check whether the target term has the correct form or that it is placed grammatically in the translation. If terminological correctness is evaluated solely by counting the occurrence of target terms in any inflection form, the evaluation becomes very easy to cheat in (purposefully or by accident): the model simply needs to add the terms in any position in the translation. This cheating problem particularly affects hard terminology constraint methods, i.e. constrained decoding and pass-through placeholders, since they will always produce the target terms, but soft constraint models are not immune to it either.

(Alam et al., 2021a) proposes multiple solutions to the cheating problem:

1. Window overlap: When a target term occurs in a translation, extract n content words surrounding the target term and check how many of those content words also occur in the n content words surrounding the same target term in a reference translation. This will reward terms that are placed similarly to the corresponding term in a reference translation.

2. Terminology-biased TER (TERm): A modified TER metric, where the edit cost is doubled for any reference word belonging to a target term.

It should be noted that both of these metrics rely on reference translations, so they are are affected by the same problem as all reference-based metrics: the single reference translation available represents only one of many possible valid translations, and many valid translations are therefore scored incorrectly. However, combined with Exact-Match Accuracy, these metrics can provide some extra information about the term accuracy of MT models.

Data for term accuracy evaluation

Evaluating term accuracy requires minimally a terminology and a collection of source language sentences which contain terms present in the terminology. This type of data is easy to obtain in theory, since monolingual data is plentiful, and there are many freely available and extensive terminology databases, such as IATE. However, test data created in this manner is artificial and may not reflect actual use cases of terminology, unless the data is carefully prepared and reviewed. Because of this, we use publicly available terminology test sets for evaluation. We found three potentially suitable test sets:

1. Annotated Tico-19 test set published for the WMT21 term task (Alam et al., 2021b).[8]

2. Test set for a case study on terminology translation for the Canadian Parliament (Knowles et al., 2023). [9]

[6] https://github.com/mahfuzibnalam/terminology_evaluation
[7] https://github.com/TommiNieminen/soft-term-constraints
[8] https://www.statmt.org/wmt21/terminology-task.html
[9] https://github.com/nrc-cnrc/PFT-ef-EAMT23

	Test sets	Base model	Term model	Only-terms model	Change: base to term
en-bg	FLORES	41.64 / 0.866	42.91 / 0.875	43.33 / 0.877	1.27 / 0.009
en-da	FLORES	45.85 / 0.865	46.71 / 0.866	47.10 / 0.865	0.86 / 0.001
en-de	WMT17,18,19+FLORES	40.55 / 0.787	40.65 / 0.787	41.60 / 0.788	0.1 / 0
en-es	WMT11,12,13+FLORES	38.20 / 0.816	37.70 / 0.814	38.06 / 0.817	-0.5 / -0.002
en-et	WMT18+FLORES	23.71 / 0.824	25.55 / 0.848	25.56 / 0.849	1.84 / 0.024
en-fi	WMT17,18,19+FLORES	26.63 / 0.862	25.91 / 0.866	25.94 / 0.866	-0.72 / 0.004
en-fr	WMT11,12,13+FLORES	35.98 / 0.798	33.68 / 0.795	34.94 / 0.805	-2.3 / -0.003
en-it	WMT09+FLORES	33.11 / 0.816	32.84 / 0.817	34.38 / 0.825	-0.27 / 0.001
en-nl	FLORES	26.49 / 0.824	27.76 / 0.826	27.11 / 0.825	1.27 / 0.002
en-lt	WMT19+FLORES	20.63 / 0.782	22.84 / 0.814	22.68 / 0.813	2.21 / 0.032
en-sv	FLORES	44.29 / 0.868	45.43 / 0.867	45.56 / 0.865	1.14 / -0.001
fi-en	WMT17,18,19+FLORES	31.70 / 0.849	30.82 / 0.845	30.96 / 0.846	-0.88 / -0.004

Table 4: General translation performance measured as BLEU/COMET. Note that the input to the term models was not annotated with terms when translating these test sets, they translated the same unannotated input as the base model. Therefore it would be expected that the term models would perform worse in this evaluation due to being further trained for another task.

3. Automotive Test Suite, an automotive corpus annotated with terms (Bergmanis and Pinnis, 2021). [10]

Out of these three, only the Tico-19 set includes term annotations on the target side, which are required by the `terminology_evaluation` script (the Tico-19 test set uses the exact formatting that the script expects, as they were both used in the WMT21 terminology shared task). The terminology in the Canadian Parliament test set appears to be fairly generic and sparse in terminology, so we decided not the use it (especially since the English to French language pair is already covered by Tico-19). For the Automotive Test Suite, we only evaluated term accuracy, using the same script as in (Bergmanis and Pinnis, 2021) in order to produce comparable results.

We do not include results for the *only-terms* model for these test sets, as all other results point to there being very little difference in performance between the *term* and *only-terms* models.

The test sets are primarily used to compare base model and term model performance to see if any improvement in term translation occurs. Although we include the results from the articles connected to these sets in our result tables (tables 5 and 6) for reference, they are not directly comparable to the results obtained with our models. First of all, the base models we use have been trained on a larger parallel corpus, which affects the COMET and BLEU metrics and may also affect the term accuracy score. Secondly, even though we use the same scripts as in the referred articles for evaluation, there may be subtle differences due to post-publication changes to the scripts.

[10] https://github.com/tilde-nlp/terminology_translation

Artificial test sets

The available test sets are relatively small and cover only a few of the language pairs for which we have trained models for, so we additionally test the models on artificial test sets which have been generated with the same method as the annotated training set. These test sets are created by concatenating the normal test sets for a language pair, annotating the concatenated file with pseudo-terms, and then generating source and target files in the .sgm format required by the `terminology_evaluation` script. One limitation of the artificial test sets is that the pseudo-terms tend to be common words and phrases, which often have only one suitable translation in the context. This means they probably overestimate the term accuracy of the base models. The results of the artificial test set evaluation are listed in table 7.

Discussion of automatic evaluation results

Automatic evaluation with both the previously published test sets and the artificial test sets clearly indicate that the continued training with terminology annotations increases terminology accuracy significantly, without degradation in overall translation quality, whether or not the source sentence contains terms. Term models consistently have

	Exact Match Accuracy	Window Overlap 1	Window 2 Overlap 2	TERm	BLEU	COMET
base	0.838	0.253	0.264	0.609	46.80	0.802
term	0.931	0.245	0.257	0.582	42.54	0.806
best in WMT21	0.974	0.359	0.352	0.625	47.69	

Table 5: Evaluation results for the Tico-19 test set from WMT21 shared terminology task (EN-FR only). Note that the best WMT21 model scores are not directly comparable due to possible differences in evaluation setup (WMT21 COMET score is omitted completely, as it is based on a different COMET model).

	Base model	Term model	TLA
en-de	29.5 / 47.6	33.2 / 95.1	33.5 / 94.0
en-et	19.8 / 40.2	22.6 / 82.5	21.0 / 87.2
en-lt	17.9 / 38.8	20.3 / 59.9	30.1 / 90.3

Table 6: BLEU scores and terminology accuracy scores for the Automotive Test Suite. TLA (Target Lemma Annotations) refers to results from Bergmanis and Pinnis (2021).

better term accuracy than base models, and term accuracy is usually very high (over 0.95 for all term models with the artificial test sets). The improvement of the term model Window Overlap scores compared to the base model scores also indicates that the placement of the terms in the output is reasonable.

One exception to the high term accuracy is the EN-LT term model, where term accuracy is fairly low with the ATS test set. This may be due to the low quality of the base model for EN-LT, which is reflected in the large disparity between the BLEU score (17.9 vs 30.1) of the base model and the model used by Bergmanis and Pinnis (2021).

In general, the term models perform better with the artificial test sets than with the Tico-19 and ATS test sets. This is probably due to the large amount of generic terms in the artificial test sets, which are easy for the model to get right. However, the term model performance still remains at a reasonably high level, and is considerably better than base model performance.

The evaluation of translation performance without terms indicates that no catastrophic forgetting takes place during the continued training. With most language pairs, the continued training even increases the BLEU score, although the COMET scores remain similar. This may be partly due to the fact that the training set for the continued training has been filtered with Bicleaner-AI, and should be of higher quality than the rest of the Tatoeba-Challenge data.

4.3 Manual evaluation

Since automatic evaluation cannot conclusively judge whether the term models improve terminology translation without degrading general translation quality, we conducted a short manual evaluation to determine the effect more reliably. The manual evaluation is conducted with the English to Finnish language direction. Finnish is a morphologically complex language, so problems in the grammaticality of the terms should be more apparent than with morphologically simpler target languages. The evaluator is an experienced professional English-to-Finnish translator, who is a native Finnish speaker.

51 sentence pairs were selected for manual evaluation from the artificial term test set. As mentioned, the artificial term test set contains a large amount of cases where the terms are obvious, i.e. there are only few realistic term translations, and therefore any decent model will likely translate the term according to the terminology. To extract interesting test cases, the evaluation set was picked from those sentences where the base model translation did not contain the required terms. These are more likely to be sentences for which the base model would struggle to produce correct terminology. From this set, 51 sentences for which the term model had produced a terminologically correct translation were randomly selected as the final manual evaluation set.

In the first phase of the manual evaluation, the evaluator was presented with the source sentences one by one, along with the base model and term model translations for each sentence in random order. The reviewer was instructed to select from three options for each pair of translations A and B: 1. translation A is better, 2. translation B is better or 3. translations A and B are equally good. The purpose of this phase was to determine whether the term model translations are noticeably inferior to the base model translations. Note that in this

	Model	Exact Match Accuracy	Window Overlap 1	Window 2 Overlap 2	TERm	BLEU	COMET
en-et	base	0.739	0.272	0.292	0.402	23.71	0.824
	only-terms	0.962	0.334	0.362	0.460	27.49	0.854
	term	0.964	0.337	0.364	0.457	27.71	0.855
en-nl	base	0.715	0.366	0.369	0.412	26.49	0.824
	only-terms	0.966	0.437	0.445	0.448	29.58	0.829
	term	0.970	0.439	0.448	0.452	29.83	0.831
en-fi	base	0.731	0.296	0.309	0.407	26.63	0.862
	only-terms	0.964	0.354	0.374	0.454	29.45	0.873
	term	0.967	0.356	0.376	0.454	29.59	0.874
en-sv	base	0.750	0.464	0.478	0.604	44.29	0.868
	only-terms	0.983	0.539	0.559	0.650	48.68	0.873
	term	0.980	0.537	0.556	0.655	48.78	0.874
en-bg	base	0.772	0.374	0.407	0.571	41.64	0.866
	only-terms	0.959	0.443	0.482	0.607	45.41	0.881
	term	0.965	0.442	0.481	0.609	45.39	0.879
en-es	base	0.750	0.364	0.388	0.512	38.20	0.816
	only-terms	0.975	0.421	0.451	0.553	40.85	0.825
	term	0.979	0.419	0.450	0.553	40.79	0.824
en-da	base	0.775	0.428	0.459	0.620	45.85	0.865
	only-terms	0.986	0.499	0.532	0.658	49.72	0.872
	term	0.987	0.495	0.531	0.656	49.57	0.871
fi-en	base	0.697	0.311	0.342	0.476	31.70	0.849
	only-terms	0.982	0.387	0.424	0.527	34.96	0.856
	term	0.982	0.386	0.424	0.528	34.85	0.855
en-fr	base	0.735	0.323	0.352	0.481	35.98	0.798
	only-terms	0.974	0.376	0.412	0.525	37.80	0.816
	term	0.978	0.375	0.410	0.524	37.57	0.815
en-it	base	0.763	0.350	0.367	0.463	33.11	0.816
	only-terms	0.960	0.410	0.440	0.520	37.38	0.834
	term	0.967	0.415	0.442	0.523	37.42	0.836
en-lt	base	0.708	0.212	0.236	0.333	20.63	0.782
	only-terms	0.961	0.277	0.308	0.386	25.06	0.821
	term	0.967	0.280	0.307	0.386	24.96	0.821
en-de	base	0.733	0.367	0.399	0.540	40.55	0.787
	only-terms	0.985	0.442	0.481	0.603	45.46	0.802
	term	0.986	0.440	0.479	0.601	45.24	0.802

Table 7: Term translation performance measured with the `terminology_evaluation` script using artificial term test sets. Pseudo-terms have been annotated in the term model input, but not in the base model input. Note that since the annotated terms occur in the reference translation, BLEU and COMET scores favour the term models. Test sets are the same as in Table 2.

phase the translator was not given details of the terms used in generating the translation, and they only ranked the sentences based on overall quality according to the normal translation industry standards. In this phase, the reviewer was also not yet informed that the evaluation concerned terminology.

Since the term model had access to terms that had been used in at least one acceptable translation (the reference translation based on which the pseudo-terms were generated), it would be expected to perform better than the base model in the first phase. Again, the purpose of this phase was not to compare the base and term model translations on even ground, but to determine whether noticeable quality degradation takes place with the term model.

In the second phase of the manual evaluation,

Source	The students gathered on the pier.
Terms	the student = uimakoululainen, pier = laituri
Target	Uimakoululaiset kokoontuivat laiturille.

Table 8: Example of the term model inflecting lemma forms of terms. The term model clearly utilizes the term information, as the Finnish translation of *the student* here means a student of a swimming school, and would be a very unlikely translation without the term information.

the evaluator was instructed to judge whether the term translations in the output of the term model were syntactically and/or semantically correct. The purpose of this phase was to determine whether the term placement in the term model output is reasonable, i.e. that the model is not cheating the automatic evaluation metric by placing the term in an incorrect place and/or in an incorrect morphological form. For each source sentence in the evaluation set, the reviewer was presented with the term model output and a list of terms that were expected to be in the output, in addition to the source sentence. For each translation, the reviewer recorded the number of terms which had been correctly used in the translation.

4.4 Results of manual evaluation

The results of the manual evaluation clearly indicate that the term model performs well, even if the target language is morphologically complex. In the first phase, the term model was ranked as performing better than base model in 20 cases, while the base model was judged to be better than the term model in 11 cases. In 20 cases, the model outputs were judged to be of equal quality. The results of the second phase also indicate that the term model performs well, with the reviewer judging 171 out of 178 terms as being correctly used. Since the morphological forms of the terms present in the output are very varied, it is clear that the model is capable of inflecting the lemma forms of the terms. Table 8 shows one example of the term model correctly inflecting several terms.

5 Energy use considerations

Training of NMT models consumes considerable amounts of energy. Strubell et al. (2019) estimate that training a *transformer-base* model of the type used in our experiments consumes 27 kWh of energy. Since we do not train from scratch but use continued training, the energy consumption of actual model training is considerably lower than the 27 kWh baseline. Unfortunately, we could not track the exact energy consumption of the experiments due to the nature of the computing infrastructure that was used (shared dual GPU in a supercomputer, where energy measurement data of the GPU includes the data for other jobs running on the same dual GPU). Based on the partial energy consumption data that we have recorded and the running times on jobs, we estimate that the continued training consumed approximately 0.35 kWh per model.

While the energy consumption of the continued training is low, using Stanza to annotate the training corpus with terminology information consumes significant amounts of energy. We estimate that the terminology annotation consumes around 5 kWh per language pair. The energy use could be minimized by switching to a less resource-intensive parser (such as `spaCy`[11]).

While the energy consumption of Bicleaner-AI is also significant, it is not included here, since we used publicly available pre-existing Bicleaner-AI scores from the Tatoeba-Challenge project.[12]

Based on a survey by Donnellan et al. (2023), the estimates above have been multiplied with a Power Usage Effectiveness (PUE) value of 1.58.

6 Conclusions

The experiments described in this article demonstrate that continued training can be used to add soft terminology constraints to pre-trained generic MT models. Automatic and manual evaluation of the model outputs clearly indicate that high levels of terminology accuracy can be achieved at a fraction of the energy cost of training a new model from scratch.

7 Acknowledgments

This work is part of the GreenNLP project, funded by the Finnish Research Council (funding agreement 353166).

References

Ailem, Melissa, Jingshu Liu, and Raheel Qader. 2021. Encouraging neural machine translation to satisfy

[11] https://spacy.io/

[12] https://github.com/Helsinki-NLP/Tatoeba-Challenge/blob/master/BicleanerScores.md

terminology constraints. In *Findings of the Association for Computational Linguistics: ACL-IJCNLP 2021*, pages 1450–1455, Online, August. Association for Computational Linguistics.

Alam, Md Mahfuz Ibn, Antonios Anastasopoulos, Laurent Besacier, James Cross, Matthias Gallé, Philipp Koehn, and Vassilina Nikoulina. 2021a. On the evaluation of machine translation for terminology consistency. *CoRR*, abs/2106.11891.

Alam, Md Mahfuz Ibn, Ivana Kvapilíková, Antonios Anastasopoulos, Laurent Besacier, Georgiana Dinu, Marcello Federico, Matthias Gallé, Kweonwoo Jung, Philipp Koehn, and Vassilina Nikoulina. 2021b. Findings of the wmt shared task on machine translation using terminologies. In *Proceedings of the Sixth Conference on Machine Translation*, pages 652–663, Online, November. Association for Computational Linguistics.

Bawden, Rachel, Nikolay Bogoychev, Ulrich Germann, Roman Grundkiewicz, Faheem Kirefu, Antonio Valerio Miceli Barone, and Alexandra Birch. 2019. The University of Edinburgh's submissions to the WMT19 news translation task. In Bojar, Ondřej, Rajen Chatterjee, Christian Federmann, Mark Fishel, Yvette Graham, Barry Haddow, Matthias Huck, Antonio Jimeno Yepes, Philipp Koehn, André Martins, Christof Monz, Matteo Negri, Aurélie Névéol, Mariana Neves, Matt Post, Marco Turchi, and Karin Verspoor, editors, *Proceedings of the Fourth Conference on Machine Translation (Volume 2: Shared Task Papers, Day 1)*, pages 103–115, Florence, Italy, August. Association for Computational Linguistics.

Bergmanis, Toms and Mārcis Pinnis. 2021. Facilitating terminology translation with target lemma annotations. In *Proceedings of the 16th Conference of the European Chapter of the Association for Computational Linguistics: Main Volume*, pages 3105–3111, Online, April. Association for Computational Linguistics.

Bogoychev, Nikolay and Pinzhen Chen. 2023. Terminology-aware translation with constrained decoding and large language model prompting. In Koehn, Philipp, Barry Haddow, Tom Kocmi, and Christof Monz, editors, *Proceedings of the Eighth Conference on Machine Translation*, pages 890–896, Singapore, December. Association for Computational Linguistics.

Dinu, Georgiana, Prashant Mathur, Marcello Federico, and Yaser Al-Onaizan. 2019. Training neural machine translation to apply terminology constraints. In *Proceedings of the 57th Annual Meeting of the Association for Computational Linguistics*, pages 3063–3068, Florence, Italy, July. Association for Computational Linguistics.

Dogru, Gokhan and Joss Moorkens. 2024. Data augmentation with translation memories for desktop machine translation fine-tuning in 3 language pairs. *The Journal of Specialised Translation*, (41):149–178, Jan.

Donnellan, Douglas, Daniel Bizo, Jacqueline Davis, Andy Lawrence, Owen Rogers, Lenny Simon, and Max Smolaks. 2023. Uptime Institute's Global Data Center Survey Results 2023. Technical report, Uptime Institute.

Dyer, Chris, Victor Chahuneau, and Noah A. Smith. 2013. A simple, fast, and effective reparameterization of IBM model 2. In Vanderwende, Lucy, Hal Daumé III, and Katrin Kirchhoff, editors, *Human Language Technologies: Conference of the North American Chapter of the Association of Computational Linguistics, Proceedings, June 9-14, 2013, Westin Peachtree Plaza Hotel, Atlanta, Georgia, USA*, pages 644–648. The Association for Computational Linguistics.

Gowda, Thamme, Zhao Zhang, Chris Mattmann, and Jonathan May. 2021. Many-to-English machine translation tools, data, and pretrained models. In *Proceedings of the 59th Annual Meeting of the Association for Computational Linguistics and the 11th International Joint Conference on Natural Language Processing: System Demonstrations*, pages 306–316, Online, August. Association for Computational Linguistics.

Goyal, Naman, Cynthia Gao, Vishrav Chaudhary, Peng-Jen Chen, Guillaume Wenzek, Da Ju, Sanjana Krishnan, Marc'Aurelio Ranzato, Francisco Guzmán, and Angela Fan. 2021. The flores-101 evaluation benchmark for low-resource and multilingual machine translation.

Hokamp, Chris and Qun Liu. 2017. Lexically constrained decoding for sequence generation using grid beam search. In *Annual Meeting of the Association for Computational Linguistics*.

Junczys-Dowmunt, Marcin, Roman Grundkiewicz, Tomasz Dwojak, Hieu Hoang, Kenneth Heafield, Tom Neckermann, Frank Seide, Ulrich Germann, Alham Fikri Aji, Nikolay Bogoychev, André F. T. Martins, and Alexandra Birch. 2018. Marian: Fast neural machine translation in C++. In *Proceedings of ACL 2018, System Demonstrations*, pages 116–121, Melbourne, Australia, July. Association for Computational Linguistics.

Knowles, Rebecca, Samuel Larkin, Marc Tessier, and Michel Simard. 2023. Terminology in neural machine translation: A case study of the Canadian Hansard. In *Proceedings of the 24th Annual Conference of the European Association for Machine Translation*, pages 481–488, Tampere, Finland, June. European Association for Machine Translation.

Kreutzer, Julia, Isaac Caswell, Lisa Wang, Ahsan Wahab, Daan van Esch, Nasanbayar Ulzii-Orshikh, Allahsera Tapo, Nishant Subramani, Artem Sokolov, Claytone Sikasote, Monang Setyawan, Supheakmungkol Sarin, Sokhar Samb, Benoît Sagot, Clara Rivera, Annette Rios, Isabel Papadimitriou, Salomey Osei, Pedro Ortiz Suarez, Iroro Orife, Kelechi

Ogueji, Andre Niyongabo Rubungo, Toan Q. Nguyen, Mathias Müller, André Müller, Shamsuddeen Hassan Muhammad, Nanda Muhammad, Ayanda Mnyakeni, Jamshidbek Mirzakhalov, Tapiwanashe Matangira, Colin Leong, Nze Lawson, Sneha Kudugunta, Yacine Jernite, Mathias Jenny, Orhan Firat, Bonaventure F. P. Dossou, Sakhile Dlamini, Nisansa de Silva, Sakine Çabuk Ballı, Stella Biderman, Alessia Battisti, Ahmed Baruwa, Ankur Bapna, Pallavi Baljekar, Israel Abebe Azime, Ayodele Awokoya, Duygu Ataman, Orevaoghene Ahia, Oghenefego Ahia, Sweta Agrawal, and Mofetoluwa Adeyemi. 2022. Quality at a glance: An audit of web-crawled multilingual datasets. *Transactions of the Association for Computational Linguistics*, 10:50–72.

Kudo, Taku and John Richardson. 2018. SentencePiece: A simple and language independent subword tokenizer and detokenizer for neural text processing. In *Proceedings of the 2018 Conference on Empirical Methods in Natural Language Processing: System Demonstrations*, pages 66–71, Brussels, Belgium, November. Association for Computational Linguistics.

Luong, Minh-Thang and Christopher Manning. 2015. Stanford neural machine translation systems for spoken language domains. In Federico, Marcello, Sebastian Stüker, and Jan Niehues, editors, *Proceedings of the 12th International Workshop on Spoken Language Translation: Evaluation Campaign*, pages 76–79, Da Nang, Vietnam, December 3-4.

Mccloskey, Michael and Neil J. Cohen. 1989. Catastrophic interference in connectionist networks: The sequential learning problem. *The Psychology of Learning and Motivation*, 24:104–169.

Michon, Elise, Josep Maria Crego, and Jean Senellart. 2020. Integrating domain terminology into neural machine translation. In *International Conference on Computational Linguistics*.

Mölder, Felix, Kim Philipp Jablonski, Brice Letcher, Michael B. Hall, Christopher H. Tomkins-Tinch, Vanessa V. Sochat, Jan Forster, Soohyun Lee, Sven O. Twardziok, Alexander Kanitz, Andreas Wilm, Manuel Holtgrewe, Sven Rahmann, Sven Nahnsen, and Johannes Köster. 2021. Sustainable data analysis with snakemake. *F1000Research*, 10:33.

Moslem, Yasmin, Rejwanul Haque, John D. Kelleher, and Andy Way. 2023a. Adaptive machine translation with large language models. In Nurminen, Mary, Judith Brenner, Maarit Koponen, Sirkku Latomaa, Mikhail Mikhailov, Frederike Schierl, Tharindu Ranasinghe, Eva Vanmassenhove, Sergi Alvarez Vidal, Nora Aranberri, Mara Nunziatini, Carla Parra Escartín, Mikel Forcada, Maja Popovic, Carolina Scarton, and Helena Moniz, editors, *Proceedings of the 24th Annual Conference of the European Association for Machine Translation*, pages 227–237, Tampere, Finland, June. European Association for Machine Translation.

Moslem, Yasmin, Gianfranco Romani, Mahdi Molaei, John D. Kelleher, Rejwanul Haque, and Andy Way. 2023b. Domain terminology integration into machine translation: Leveraging large language models. In *Proceedings of the Eighth Conference on Machine Translation*, pages 902–911, Singapore, December. Association for Computational Linguistics.

Neubig, Graham and Junjie Hu. 2018. Rapid adaptation of neural machine translation to new languages. In Riloff, Ellen, David Chiang, Julia Hockenmaier, and Jun'ichi Tsujii, editors, *Proceedings of the 2018 Conference on Empirical Methods in Natural Language Processing*, pages 875–880, Brussels, Belgium, October-November. Association for Computational Linguistics.

Post, Matt. 2018. A call for clarity in reporting BLEU scores. In *Proceedings of the Third Conference on Machine Translation: Research Papers*, pages 186–191, Belgium, Brussels, October. Association for Computational Linguistics.

Qi, Peng, Yuhao Zhang, Yuhui Zhang, Jason Bolton, and Christopher D. Manning. 2020. Stanza: A Python natural language processing toolkit for many human languages. In *Proceedings of the 58th Annual Meeting of the Association for Computational Linguistics: System Demonstrations*.

Rei, Ricardo, Craig Stewart, Ana C Farinha, and Alon Lavie. 2020. COMET: A neural framework for MT evaluation. In Webber, Bonnie, Trevor Cohn, Yulan He, and Yang Liu, editors, *Proceedings of the 2020 Conference on Empirical Methods in Natural Language Processing (EMNLP)*, pages 2685–2702, Online, November. Association for Computational Linguistics.

Semenov, Kirill, Vilém Zouhar, Tom Kocmi, Dongdong Zhang, Wangchunshu Zhou, and Yuchen Eleanor Jiang. 2023. Findings of the WMT 2023 shared task on machine translation with terminologies. In Koehn, Philipp, Barry Haddow, Tom Kocmi, and Christof Monz, editors, *Proceedings of the Eighth Conference on Machine Translation*, pages 663–671, Singapore, December. Association for Computational Linguistics.

Strubell, Emma, Ananya Ganesh, and Andrew McCallum. 2019. Energy and policy considerations for deep learning in NLP. In Korhonen, Anna, David Traum, and Lluís Màrquez, editors, *Proceedings of the 57th Annual Meeting of the Association for Computational Linguistics*, pages 3645–3650, Florence, Italy, July. Association for Computational Linguistics.

Tiedemann, Jörg and Santhosh Thottingal. 2020. OPUS-MT — Building open translation services for the World. In *Proceedings of the 22nd Annual Conferenec of the European Association for Machine Translation (EAMT)*, Lisbon, Portugal.

Tiedemann, Jörg, 2009. *News from OPUS - A Collection of Multilingual Parallel Corpora with Tools and Interfaces*, volume V, pages 237–248.

Tiedemann, Jörg. 2020. The Tatoeba Translation Challenge – Realistic data sets for low resource and multilingual MT. In *Proceedings of the Fifth Conference on Machine Translation*, pages 1174–1182, Online, November. Association for Computational Linguistics.

Zaragoza-Bernabeu, Jaume, Gema Ramírez-Sánchez, Marta Bañón, and Sergio Ortiz Rojas. "2022". "bicleaner AI: Bicleaner goes neural". In *"Proceedings of the Thirteenth Language Resources and Evaluation Conference"*, pages "824–831", "Marseille, France", June. "European Language Resources Association".

Leveraging Synthetic Monolingual Data for Fuzzy-Match Augmentation in Neural Machine Translation: A Preliminary Study

Thomas Moerman and **Arda Tezcan**
Language and Translation Technology Team (LT³)
Ghent University, Belgium
{thomas.moerman, arda.tezcan}@ugent.be

1 Background and Methodology

Recent work has demonstrated that specialized neural machine translation (NMT) models, as well as Large Language Models (LLMs), can utilize fuzzy matches (FMs) (i.e., similar translations for a given source sentence) effectively to produce translations of higher quality (Xu et al., 2020; Tezcan et al., 2021; Moslem et al., 2023).

Earlier studies have shown that FM-augmentation is especially useful in domain-specific scenarios where large bilingual datasets are available (Bulté and Tezcan, 2019; Xu et al., 2020). A more recent study (Tezcan et al., Under Revision) further demonstrated the effectiveness of FM-augmentation in settings where this approach alone is not helpful due to the availability of limited bilingual data sets by using additional monolingual data available in the target language through back-translation (BT) (Sennrich et al., 2015; Edunov et al., 2018) and subsequently applying the Neural Fuzzy Repair (NFR) technique for FM-augmentation, which relies on concatenating source sentences with the translations FMs (Tezcan et al., 2021).

This study further investigates the usefulness of FM-augmentation for NMT in domain-specific scenarios where limited bilingual datasets are available without any additional monolingual datasets. We aim to bridge this gap by generating additional monolingual data in the target language using an LLM and employing back-translation to generate corresponding sentences in the source text, as also proposed by Moslem et al. (2022). Additionally, we use the synthetic source/target sentence pairs for FM-augmentation in the context of specialized NMT systems.

In this preliminary study, we use the DGT Translation Memory (DGT-TM) of the European Commission's translation service[1], for English→French, covering European legislation texts. The dataset includes 300,000 sentence pairs for NMT training and 2,000 for validation and testing. The choice of this data set is two-fold: (i) it has been demonstrated that the NFR approach itself did not yield performance improvements when using this data set size obtained from the DGT-TM (Bulté and Tezcan, 2019), and (ii) the NFR approach yielded clear improvements when the training data was increased through back-translating the additionally available (high-quality) monolingual data in the target language (Tezcan et al., Under Revision).

The proposed approach consists of three main steps:

1. **Synthetic Data Generation:** First, synthetic sentences in the target language (French) are produced using the Mistral-7b-instruct-v0.2 model (Jiang et al., 2023), following a prompt designed to achieve thematic coherence (Veselovsky et al., 2023). This stage employs the vLLM library[2], which utilizes paged attention (Kwon et al., 2023). Further details on the synthetic data generation process are provided in Appendix A.1.

2. **Back-translation:** Next, these synthetic sentences are back-translated into the source language using a pre-trained NMT system with the same training data (300K sentence pairs), only trained in the reverse language direction (FR→EN). The synthetically generated bilin-

[1] https://opus.nlpl.eu/DGT/corpus/version/DGT
[2] https://github.com/vllm-project/vllm

Proceedings of the First International Workshop on Knowledge-Enhanced Machine Translation, pages 34–39
June 27, 2024 ©2024 European Association for Machine Translation

gual data set is then merged with the original training data.

3. **FM Augmentation:** This step involves using the NFR approach (Tezcan et al., 2021), which retrieves the highest FM for each source sentence from the merged training data and uses its translation for source-augmentation in each data partition, where FM similarity is measured by cosine similarity between sentence embeddings[3].

To test the usefulness of the proposed approach in different data settings, the training data was incrementally increased through synthetic data generation in the target language from 300K sentences (the same size as the bilingual data set) to 1.5M sentences (five times larger than the bilingual data set size).

We primarily utilized the default settings of the transformer architecture as implemented in OpenNMT[4] (Klein et al., 2017) with early stopping. SacreBLEU (Post, 2018), ChrF (Popović, 2015) and COMET (Rei et al., 2020) were used to automatically assess the MT performance.

2 Preliminary Results

The preliminary results of this ongoing study highlight several key findings:

- Applying FM-augmentation (NFR) on the original bilingual training data does not yield better translation performance against the standard (baseline) NMT system, confirming previous findings (Bulté and Tezcan, 2019).
- Utilizing additional synthetic training data without FM-augmentation, namely synthetically generated monolingual data in the target language via Mistral and corresponding source sentences produced through BT, achieves results comparable to the baseline NMT system.
- Using FM-augmentation in combination with synthetic data generation improves results across all additional monolingual data set sizes, outperforming both the baseline and NFR systems.
- The proposed approach achieves optimal improvements when the synthetically generated monolingual data set size is twice (BLEU and ChrF) or four times (COMET) that of the original bilingual data set. However, performance declines with the addition of larger synthetic data sets.
- The optimal improvements when using the proposed approach are observed to be up to +1.44 BLEU points compared to the baseline NMT system and +1.59 BLEU points compared to the NFR system while showing statistically significant improvements across all three metrics (bootstrap resampling with $p < 0.05$).

For an overview of the automated evaluation results for each system tested in this study, please see Appendix A.3.

Preliminary results from this ongoing work suggest that in this specific setting, the proposed approach, consisting of generating (i) synthetic monolingual data in the target language via an LLM, (ii) synthetic source sentences through back-translation, and (iii) applying NFR, could be an effective strategy for enhancing the performance of specialized NMT systems.

The effectiveness of the proposed approach prompts further investigation into whether (i) similar observations can be made in different data settings (especially in lower-resource settings), domains and language directions; and (ii) the MT performance can be further enhanced through alternative synthetic data generation strategies (both in the target and source language) and/or with increasing amounts of such additional synthetic data.

Acknowledgements

The computational resources (Stevin Supercomputer Infrastructure) and services used in this work were provided by the VSC (Flemish Supercomputer Center), which is funded by Ghent University, FWO and the Flemish Government department EWI.

References

Bulté, Bram and Arda Tezcan. 2019. Neural fuzzy repair: Integrating fuzzy matches into neural machine translation. In *Proceedings of the 57th Annual Meeting of the Association for Computational Linguistics*, pages 1800–1809, Florence, Italy, July. Association for Computational Linguistics.

Edunov, Sergey, Myle Ott, Michael Auli, and David Grangier. 2018. Understanding back-translation at

[3]https://github.com/lt3/nfr
[4]https://github.com/OpenNMT/OpenNMT-py-v3.5.1

scale. In Riloff, Ellen, David Chiang, Julia Hockenmaier, and Jun'ichi Tsujii, editors, *Proceedings of the 2018 Conference on Empirical Methods in Natural Language Processing*, pages 489–500, Brussels, Belgium, October-November. Association for Computational Linguistics.

Jiang, Albert Q., Alexandre Sablayrolles, Arthur Mensch, Chris Bamford, Devendra Singh Chaplot, Diego de las Casas, Florian Bressand, Gianna Lengyel, Guillaume Lample, Lucile Saulnier, Lélio Renard Lavaud, Marie-Anne Lachaux, Pierre Stock, Teven Le Scao, Thibaut Lavril, Thomas Wang, Timothée Lacroix, and William El Sayed. 2023. Mistral 7b.

Klein, Guillaume, Yoon Kim, Yuntian Deng, Jean Senellart, and Alexander M Rush. 2017. OpenNMT: Open-source toolkit for neural machine translation. *Computing Research Repository*, arXiv:1701.02810.

Kwon, Woosuk, Zhuohan Li, Siyuan Zhuang, Ying Sheng, Lianmin Zheng, Cody Hao Yu, Joseph E. Gonzalez, Hao Zhang, and Ion Stoica. 2023. Efficient memory management for large language model serving with pagedattention. In *Proceedings of the ACM SIGOPS 29th Symposium on Operating Systems Principles*.

Moslem, Yasmin, Rejwanul Haque, John Kelleher, and Andy Way. 2022. Domain-specific text generation for machine translation. In Duh, Kevin and Francisco Guzmán, editors, *Proceedings of the 15th biennial conference of the Association for Machine Translation in the Americas (Volume 1: Research Track)*, pages 14–30, Orlando, USA, September. Association for Machine Translation in the Americas.

Moslem, Yasmin, Rejwanul Haque, John D. Kelleher, and Andy Way. 2023. Adaptive machine translation with large language models. In Nurminen, Mary, Judith Brenner, Maarit Koponen, Sirkku Latomaa, Mikhail Mikhailov, Frederike Schierl, Tharindu Ranasinghe, Eva Vanmassenhove, Sergi Alvarez Vidal, Nora Aranberri, Mara Nunziatini, Carla Parra Escartín, Mikel Forcada, Maja Popovic, Carolina Scarton, and Helena Moniz, editors, *Proceedings of the 24th Annual Conference of the European Association for Machine Translation*, pages 227–237, Tampere, Finland, June. European Association for Machine Translation.

Popović, Maja. 2015. chrF: character n-gram F-score for automatic MT evaluation. In Bojar, Ondřej, Rajan Chatterjee, Christian Federmann, Barry Haddow, Chris Hokamp, Matthias Huck, Varvara Logacheva, and Pavel Pecina, editors, *Proceedings of the Tenth Workshop on Statistical Machine Translation*, pages 392–395, Lisbon, Portugal, September. Association for Computational Linguistics.

Post, Matt. 2018. A call for clarity in reporting BLEU scores. In *Proceedings of the Third Conference on Machine Translation: Research Papers*, pages 186–191, Belgium, Brussels, October. Association for Computational Linguistics.

Rei, Ricardo, Craig Stewart, Ana C Farinha, and Alon Lavie. 2020. COMET: A neural framework for MT evaluation. In Webber, Bonnie, Trevor Cohn, Yulan He, and Yang Liu, editors, *Proceedings of the 2020 Conference on Empirical Methods in Natural Language Processing (EMNLP)*, pages 2685–2702, Online, November. Association for Computational Linguistics.

Sennrich, Rico, Barry Haddow, and Alexandra Birch. 2015. Improving neural machine translation models with monolingual data. *arXiv preprint arXiv:1511.06709*.

Tezcan, Arda, Bram Bulté, and Bram Vanroy. 2021. Towards a better integration of fuzzy matches in neural machine translation through data augmentation. *Informatics*, 8(1).

Tezcan, Arda, Alina Skidanova, and Thomas Moerman. Under Revision. Improving fuzzy match augmented neural machine translation through synthetic data.

Veselovsky, Veniamin, Manoel Horta Ribeiro, Akhil Arora, Martin Josifoski, Ashton Anderson, and Robert West. 2023. Generating faithful synthetic data with large language models: A case study in computational social science.

Xu, Jitao, Josep Crego, and Jean Senellart. 2020. Boosting neural machine translation with similar translations. In Jurafsky, Dan, Joyce Chai, Natalie Schluter, and Joel Tetreault, editors, *Proceedings of the 58th Annual Meeting of the Association for Computational Linguistics*, pages 1580–1590, Online, July. Association for Computational Linguistics.

A Appendix

A.1 Synthetic Data Generation

Sampling Parameters for Mistral-7b-instruct-v0.2

The specific sampling parameters differing from default values are outlined below. For details on default parameter settings, please refer to the vLLM library documentation at https://docs.vllm.ai/en/latest/dev/sampling_params.html. These parameter adjustments were adopted from the findings in Moslem et al. (2022).

Parameter	Value
Top-p	0.95
Top-k	50
Frequency Penalty	0.5
Repetition Penalty	1.2
Max Tokens	400

Table 1: Sampling parameters for Mistral-7b-instruct-v0.2

Prompt Design

Table 2 outlines the specific prompt design utilized for generating French sentences, highlighting the instruction and the examples given to the language model and the response given to that prompt.

A.2 FM-augmentation

See Table 3 for an example of FM retrieval and source augmentation.

A.3 Translation Performance

See Table 4 for all metrics (BLEU, ChrF and COMET) and Table 5 for the performance of the back-translation model.

- **Baseline** refers to the standard NMT system trained on the original 300k bilingual data.
- **Baseline + BT(1:X)** refers to the non-augmented NMT system, using additional synthetically generated target sentences (through LLM) and their translations in the source language (through back-translation), where X indicates the ratio of synthetic to original data.
- **NFR** refers to the system trained on the original bilingual data after applying FM-augmentation.
- **BT 1:X + NFR** refers to the FM-augmented NMT model, using additional synthetically generated target sentences (through LLM) and their translations in the source language (through back-translation) with Neural Fuzzy Repair, where X indicates the ratio of synthetic to original data (the proposed approach in this study).

Prompt (French)	**LLM Response**
[INST] Votre tâche consiste à générer des phrases françaises similaires en termes de domaine et de style aux exemples fournis ci-dessous. Exemples de phrases : 1. Les cotisations des membres pour l'exercice au cours duquel ils deviennent membres du Conseil oléicole international sont exigibles à la date où ils deviennent membres. 2. Au vu de ces circonstances, la Suède a été confrontée à des difficultés temporaires d'approvisionnement général en semences de plantes fourragères de printemps et en semences de céréales de printemps, et ces difficultés ne devraient pas se dissiper. 3. La contribution de chaque État membre participant auprès duquel une contribution est demandée est proportionnelle à la part du RNB de cet État membre dans le total des RNB des États membres participants auprès desquels une contribution est demandée. 4. L'article 199 ter est remplacé par le texte suivant: 5. Dans les limites du montant fixé, l'organe de la société habilité à cet effet décide, le cas échéant, d'augmenter le capital souscrit. Veuillez générer 10 nouvelles phrases françaises basées sur les exemples ci-dessus. [/INST]	1. Les impôts des nouveaux membres du Comité céréalier international sont dus à la date où ils rejoignent ce comité. 2. En raison de ces circonstances, la Norvège a confronté des difficultés temporaires d'approvisionnement général en graines de fourrages d'été et en graines de blé d'été, et ces difficultés ne devraient pas disparaître. 3. La contribution de chaque État membre participant, où une contribution est demandée, est proportionnelle à la part du Fonds communautaire de ce pays membre dans le total des Fonds communautaires des États membres participants where a contribution is requested. 4. L'article 200 quater est remplacé par le texte suivant : 5. Dans les limites du montant fixé, l'organe de la société autorisé à cette fin décide, le cas échéant, d'augmenter le capital souscrit. 6. Les cotisations des nouveaux membres du Conseil oléicole européen sont exigibles à la date où ils deviennent membres. 7. En raison des circonstances actuelles, la Finlande a été confrontée à des difficultés temporaires d'approvisionnement général en graines de fourrages hiver et en graines de blé d'hiver, et ces difficultés ne devraient pas se résoudre. 8. La contribution de chaque État membre participant où une contribution est demandée est proportionnelle à la part du Fonds communautaire de ce pays membre dans le total des Fonds communautaires des États membres participants where a contribution is demanded. 9. L'article 201 quinquiès est modifié pour devenir le texte ci-après : 10. Dans les limites du montant prévu, l'organe de la société compétent en matière de cession de droits décide, si nécessaire, d'augmenter le capital souscrit.

Table 2: Prompt used for generating domain-specific French sentences alongside the LLM-generated response.

S	Debt, breakdown by residual maturity
$score$	0.9812
FM_S	Debt, breakdown by **initial** maturity
FM_T	Dette, ventilation par échéance **initiale**
S'	Debt, breakdown by residual maturity $< sep >$ Dette, ventilation par échéance initiale
T	Dette, ventilation par échéance résiduelle

Table 3: An example of FM retrieval and source augmentation (S') for a given source sentence (S) for the EN→FR language direction, with the translation 'T'. 'FM_S' and 'FM_T' refer to the source and target sides of the retrieved FM, respectively. The sentence similarity score is indicated as '$score$'.

Configuration	BLEU	ChrF	COMET
Baseline	45.76	64.97	79.75
BT 1:1	45.69	65.11	80.20
BT 1:2	45.79	65.26	80.44
BT 1:3	44.96	64.70	80.43
BT 1:4	44.57	64.44	80.31
BT 1:5	45.19	64.89	80.64
NFR	45.61	64.91	79.90
BT 1:1 + NFR	47.14	65.91	80.76
BT 1:2 + NFR	**47.20**	**66.03**	80.76
BT 1:3 + NFR	47.03	65.90	80.90
BT 1:4 + NFR	46.87	65.80	**80.91**
BT 1:5 + NFR	45.90	65.52	80.88

Table 4: Automated evaluation of the different NMT systems.

System	BLEU	ChrF	COMET
FR→EN	47.76	65.19	80.69

Table 5: Automated evaluation of the back-translation (NMT) model, which is trained on the original parallel data set in reverse language direction and evaluated on the reversed test set.

Can True Zero-shot Methods with Large Language Models be Adopted for Sign Language Machine Translation?

Euan McGill
Universitat Pompeu Fabra
Barcelona, Spain
euan.mcgill@upf.edu

Horacio Saggion
Universitat Pompeu Fabra
Barcelona, Spain
horacio.saggion@upf.edu

1 Introduction

'Long-tail' or low resource languages are spoken by communities which are often left out of technological advancements, and therefore further endanger a given language's survival (Kornai, 2013; Joshi et al., 2020). They can be identified in typological resources such as Ethnologue (Eberhard et al., 2024) with metrics such as Language Vitality and Digital Language Support (Simons et al., 2022). The possibility of generating and translating text into these languages may enable the empowerment of these communities and enduring linguistic diversity.

The rise of data-intensive and large language model (LLM)-based language technologies for tasks like machine translation (MT), automatic speech recognition, and named entity recognition has enabled the inclusion of low-resource spoken languages in these technologies. Within MT, practical multilingual *few-shot* and *zero-shot* models have been created for nearly all of the $1,500$ languages[1] where there is text data that can be mined from the web (Bapna et al., 2022; Goyal et al., 2022; Federmann et al., 2022; Maillard et al., 2023; FitzGerald et al., 2023; Ruder et al., 2023) and also multimodal data (Bugliarello et al., 2022).

For the other $c.6,000$ languages, however, there exists either little or no digital presence. Resources may be confined to restricted dictionaries or wordlists, for example gathered in linguistic fieldwork studies.

As shown in Figure 1, Ethnologue's 159 documented Sign Languages (SLs) are all digitally low-resource. They cover the full spectrum of Language Vitality - but no SL has a Digital Language Support status higher than 'Emerging[2]'. SLs are characterised by multimodality (Bragg et al., 2019) and there is a lack of agreement on standardising textual SL data (Cormier et al., 2016; De Sisto et al., 2022), if there is textual data at all[3].

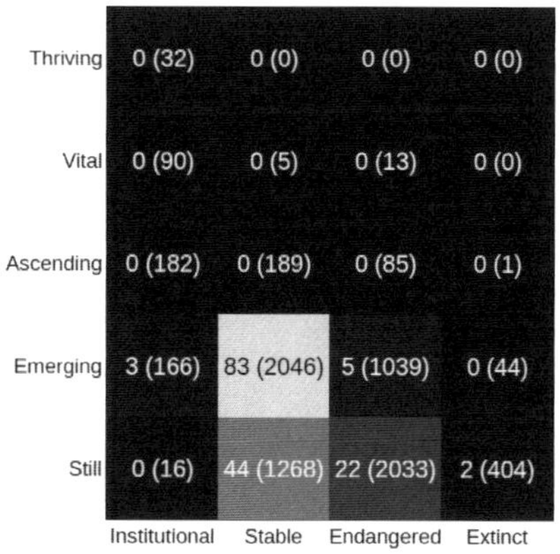

Figure 1: Labelled heatmap of the 159 SLs categorised by Language Vitality (x-axis) and Digital Language Support (y-axis). In brackets, figures for all Ethnologue languages

The unique challenge of SL data means that the methods mentioned so far may be unsuitable. Most rely on text mined from the web, while the digital resources available for SLs are usually in image or video format. In addition, other methods such as data augmentation have been attempted but have reached a performance ceiling because of the lack of parallel data available and the prospect of real, large-scale data collection efforts (De Coster et al., 2023).

[1] https://newsletter.ruder.io/p/true-zero-shot-mt provides an overview of current efforts towards true-zero shot machine translation (MT) for extremely low resource languages, and serves as the inspiration for this investigation

[2] "...some content in digital form and/or encoding tools"

[3] Moryossef (2021) characterises SLs as *extremely* low resource languages

Proceedings of the First International Workshop on Knowledge-Enhanced Machine Translation, pages 40–43
June 27, 2024 ©2024 European Association for Machine Translation

1.1 True zero shot methods

A recent work, **"Machine Translation from One Book (MTOB)"** (Tanzer et al., 2024), creates a benchmark which shows that LLMs show promise in learning sequences of a language which does not exist on the web, and is therefore completely opaque to any LLM's training data.

The authors use a *true zero-shot* approach (see also Zhang et al. (2024a) and Zhang et al. (2024b)) enabled by advances in LLMs whose prompting context window can be sufficiently long to contain book-length resources - such as a descriptive linguistic fieldwork grammar - and even multimodal data in text, audio and video (*e.g.* Gemini 1.5 Pro (Reid et al., 2024)).

It is hoped that leveraging the techniques of MTOB can be transferable to MT involving SLs (SLMT). The rest of this extended abstract describes the additional challenges foreseen by attempting this, and some methodological choices that will need to be made.

2 Resources, Challenges and Evaluation

Resources: According to repositories like Glottolog[4] (Hammarström et al., 2024), there appears to be a broad range of language grammars, dictionaries and textbooks describing numerous SLs - at least as many as for spoken languages (Zhang et al., 2024b). Resources not yet made publicly available on the web would be the most important to analyse, in order to appraise the MTOB approach on a SL unseen to any LLM training. It would also be important to adopt techniques for LM efficiency in low-resource scenarios (Warstadt et al., 2023).

Representations: Decisions around the appropriate representation in text, or even the medium itself (visual *versus* textual) are perhaps the most important that need to be made for the proposed approach.

SL grammars are likely to use glosses[5] to represent signs in examples and glossaries as well as in parallel corpora with continuous SL data[6]. Otherwise, a notation system such as SignWriting[7] could be used. It is compatible with the MTOB approach, as its characters are encoded in Unicode or translatable to ASCII (Jiang et al., 2023).

[4]e.g. https://glottolog.org/resource/languoid/id/cata1241 as an example for Catalan Sign Language

[5]A lexical representation based on a spoken language

[6]https://how2sign.github.io/related_datasets.html

[7]https://www.sutton-signwriting.io/

As for the medium - the multimodality of SLs alongside the ability of models like Gemini 1.5 Pro (Reid et al., 2024) to interpret visual, audio, or text data make a *true zero-shot* study a complex, but exciting prospect.

Evaluation: Model output in MTOB and other *few* and *zero-shot* methods has been evaluated with automatic metrics solely on text. Character based metrics such as CHrF (Popović, 2015; Bapna et al., 2022; Ruder et al., 2023), have been used for languages which are low resource, do not have clear token boundaries, or using non-romanised characters (Tanzer et al., 2024). These metrics may be suitable for SLs which are low resource, and may be notated in a system like SignWriting.

It may be possible to use BLEU (Papineni et al., 2002), standard in MT, but is known to be problematic in languages where there is only one reference translation. In addition, if SL data is presented as linear glosses, BLEU (which relies on tokenised text) may be an appropriate metric.

Further considerations: The principal users and guardians of SLs, and their related technologies, is the Deaf and Hard-of-Hearing (DHH) community. As such, it is essential to work under the principle of "nothing about us without us" (Vandeghinste et al., 2023). DHH stakeholders must consent to this technology being investigated, the use of SL data and resources, as well as being involved in the research itself.

3 Call to arms

In summary, recent research has shown that it is possible to show multimodal LLMs, within prompts, entire language descriptions with examples from book-length texts. Then, they have been shown to be able to provide translations between English and a language which has never been seen by the LLM.

This extended abstract shows the potential of extending this methodology to SLs, and intends to begin a discussion towards experimenting in LLMs with long prompt windows and SL data.

However, there remains the following open questions in order to develop this technology: **(1)** Which language pairs to target?, **(2)** How to incorporate non-text modalities?, **(3)** How to integrate image content in linguistic texts into multimodal models?, **(4)** What are the computing resources required to conduct this research?, **(5)** How to integrate the DHH community at each stage?

Acknowledgements

This work is part of Maria de Maeztu Units of Excellence Programme CEX2021-001195-M, funded by MCIN/AEI /10.13039/501100011033

References

Bapna, Ankur, Isaac Caswell, Julia Kreutzer, Orhan Firat, Daan van Esch, Aditya Siddhant, Mengmeng Niu, Pallavi Baljekar, Xavier Garcia, Wolfgang Macherey, Theresa Breiner, Vera Axelrod, Jason Riesa, Yuan Cao, Mia Xu Chen, Klaus Macherey, Maxim Krikun, Pidong Wang, Alexander Gutkin, Apurva Shah, Yanping Huang, Zhifeng Chen, Yonghui Wu, and Macduff Hughes. 2022. Building machine translation systems for the next thousand languages.

Bragg, Danielle, Oscar Koller, Mary Bellard, Larwan Berke, Patrick Boudreault, Annelies Braffort, Naomi Caselli, Matt Huenerfauth, Hernisa Kacorri, Tessa Verhoef, Christian Vogler, and Meredith Ringel Morris. 2019. Sign Language Recognition, Generation, and Translation: An Interdisciplinary Perspective. In *The 21st International ACM SIGACCESS Conference on Computers and Accessibility*, ASSETS '19, page 16–31, New York, NY, USA. Association for Computing Machinery.

Bugliarello, Emanuele, Fangyu Liu, Jonas Pfeiffer, Siva Reddy, Desmond Elliott, Edoardo Maria Ponti, and Ivan Vulić. 2022. Iglue: A benchmark for transfer learning across modalities, tasks, and languages. In *International Conference on Machine Learning*, pages 2370–2392. PMLR.

Cormier, Kearsy, Onno Crasborn, and Richard Bank. 2016. Digging into signs: Emerging annotation standards for sign language corpora. In Efthimiou, Eleni, Stavroula-Evita Fotinea, Thomas Hanke, Julie A. Hochgesang, Jette Kristoffersen, and Johanna Mesch, editors, *Proceedings of the LREC2016 7th Workshop on the Representation and Processing of Sign Languages: Corpus Mining*, pages 35–40, Portorož, Slovenia, May. European Language Resources Association (ELRA).

De Coster, Mathieu, Dimitar Shterionov, Mieke Van Herreweghe, and Joni Dambre. 2023. Machine translation from signed to spoken languages: State of the art and challenges. *Universal Access in the Information Society*, pages 1–27.

De Sisto, Mirella, Vincent Vandeghinste, Santiago Egea Gómez, Mathieu De Coster, Dimitar Shterionov, and Horacio Saggion. 2022. Challenges with sign language datasets for sign language recognition and translation. In *Proceedings of the Thirteenth Language Resources and Evaluation Conference*, pages 2478–2487, Marseille, France, June. European Language Resources Association.

Eberhard, David M., Gary F. Simons, and Charles D. Fennig. 2024. Ethnologue: Languages of the World. Twenty-seventh edition.

Federmann, Christian, Tom Kocmi, and Ying Xin. 2022. NTREX-128 – news test references for MT evaluation of 128 languages. In Ahuja, Kabir, Antonios Anastasopoulos, Barun Patra, Graham Neubig, Monojit Choudhury, Sandipan Dandapat, Sunayana Sitaram, and Vishrav Chaudhary, editors, *Proceedings of the First Workshop on Scaling Up Multilingual Evaluation*, pages 21–24, Online, November. Association for Computational Linguistics.

FitzGerald, Jack, Christopher Hench, Charith Peris, Scott Mackie, Kay Rottmann, Ana Sanchez, Aaron Nash, Liam Urbach, Vishesh Kakarala, Richa Singh, Swetha Ranganath, Laurie Crist, Misha Britan, Wouter Leeuwis, Gokhan Tur, and Prem Natarajan. 2023. MASSIVE: A 1M-example multilingual natural language understanding dataset with 51 typologically-diverse languages. In Rogers, Anna, Jordan Boyd-Graber, and Naoaki Okazaki, editors, *Proceedings of the 61st Annual Meeting of the Association for Computational Linguistics (Volume 1: Long Papers)*, pages 4277–4302, Toronto, Canada, July. Association for Computational Linguistics.

Goyal, Naman, Cynthia Gao, Vishrav Chaudhary, Peng-Jen Chen, Guillaume Wenzek, Da Ju, Sanjana Krishnan, Marc'Aurelio Ranzato, Francisco Guzmán, and Angela Fan. 2022. The Flores-101 evaluation benchmark for low-resource and multilingual machine translation. *Transactions of the Association for Computational Linguistics*, 10:522–538.

Hammarström, Harald, Robert Forkel, Martin Haspelmath, and Sebastian Bank. 2024. Glottolog 5.0.

Jiang, Zifan, Amit Moryossef, Mathias Müller, and Sarah Ebling. 2023. Machine translation between spoken languages and signed languages represented in SignWriting. In Vlachos, Andreas and Isabelle Augenstein, editors, *Findings of the Association for Computational Linguistics: EACL 2023*, pages 1706–1724, Dubrovnik, Croatia, May. Association for Computational Linguistics.

Joshi, Pratik, Sebastin Santy, Amar Budhiraja, Kalika Bali, and Monojit Choudhury. 2020. The state and fate of linguistic diversity and inclusion in the NLP world. In Jurafsky, Dan, Joyce Chai, Natalie Schluter, and Joel Tetreault, editors, *Proceedings of the 58th Annual Meeting of the Association for Computational Linguistics*, pages 6282–6293, Online, July. Association for Computational Linguistics.

Kornai, András. 2013. Digital language death. *PloS one*, 8(10):e77056.

Maillard, Jean, Cynthia Gao, Elahe Kalbassi, Kaushik Ram Sadagopan, Vedanuj Goswami, Philipp Koehn, Angela Fan, and Francisco Guzman. 2023. Small data, big impact: Leveraging minimal data for effective machine translation. In Rogers, Anna, Jordan Boyd-Graber, and Naoaki Okazaki, editors, *Proceedings of the 61st Annual Meeting of the Association for Computational Linguistics (Volume 1: Long Papers)*, pages 2740–2756, Toronto, Canada, July. Association for Computational Linguistics.

Moryossef, Amit, Kayo Yin, Graham Neubig, and Yoav Goldberg. 2021. Data augmentation for sign language gloss translation. In Shterionov, Dimitar, editor, *Proceedings of the 1st International Workshop on Automatic Translation for Signed and Spoken Languages (AT4SSL)*, pages 1–11, Virtual, August. Association for Machine Translation in the Americas.

Papineni, Kishore, Salim Roukos, Todd Ward, and Wei-Jing Zhu. 2002. Bleu: a method for automatic evaluation of machine translation. In Isabelle, Pierre, Eugene Charniak, and Dekang Lin, editors, *Proceedings of the 40th Annual Meeting of the Association for Computational Linguistics*, pages 311–318, Philadelphia, Pennsylvania, USA, July. Association for Computational Linguistics.

Popović, Maja. 2015. chrF: character n-gram F-score for automatic MT evaluation. In Bojar, Ondřej, Rajan Chatterjee, Christian Federmann, Barry Haddow, Chris Hokamp, Matthias Huck, Varvara Logacheva, and Pavel Pecina, editors, *Proceedings of the Tenth Workshop on Statistical Machine Translation*, pages 392–395, Lisbon, Portugal, September. Association for Computational Linguistics.

Reid, Machel, Nikolay Savinov, Denis Teplyashin, Dmitry Lepikhin, Timothy Lillicrap, Jean-baptiste Alayrac, Radu Soricut, Angeliki Lazaridou, Orhan Firat, Julian Schrittwieser, et al. 2024. Gemini 1.5: Unlocking multimodal understanding across millions of tokens of context. *arXiv preprint arXiv:2403.05530*.

Ruder, Sebastian, Jonathan Clark, Alexander Gutkin, Mihir Kale, Min Ma, Massimo Nicosia, Shruti Rijhwani, Parker Riley, Jean-Michel Sarr, Xinyi Wang, John Wieting, Nitish Gupta, Anna Katanova, Christo Kirov, Dana Dickinson, Brian Roark, Bidisha Samanta, Connie Tao, David Adelani, Vera Axelrod, Isaac Caswell, Colin Cherry, Dan Garrette, Reeve Ingle, Melvin Johnson, Dmitry Panteleev, and Partha Talukdar. 2023. XTREME-UP: A user-centric scarce-data benchmark for under-represented languages. In Bouamor, Houda, Juan Pino, and Kalika Bali, editors, *Findings of the Association for Computational Linguistics: EMNLP 2023*, pages 1856–1884, Singapore, December. Association for Computational Linguistics.

Simons, Gary F., Abbey L. L. Thomas, and Chad K. K. White. 2022. Assessing digital language support on a global scale. In Calzolari, Nicoletta, Chu-Ren Huang, Hansaem Kim, James Pustejovsky, Leo Wanner, Key-Sun Choi, Pum-Mo Ryu, Hsin-Hsi Chen, Lucia Donatelli, Heng Ji, Sadao Kurohashi, Patrizia Paggio, Nianwen Xue, Seokhwan Kim, Younggyun Hahm, Zhong He, Tony Kyungil Lee, Enrico Santus, Francis Bond, and Seung-Hoon Na, editors, *Proceedings of the 29th International Conference on Computational Linguistics*, pages 4299–4305, Gyeongju, Republic of Korea, October. International Committee on Computational Linguistics.

Tanzer, Garrett, Mirac Suzgun, Eline Visser, Dan Jurafsky, and Luke Melas-Kyriazi. 2024. A benchmark for learning to translate a new language from one grammar book.

Vandeghinste, Vincent, Dimitar Shterionov, Mirella De Sisto, Aoife Brady, Mathieu De Coster, Lorraine Leeson, Josep Blat, Frankie Picron, Marcello Paolo Scipioni, Aditya Parikh, Louis ten Bosch, John O'Flaherty, Joni Dambre, Jorn Rijckaert, Bram Vanroy, Victor Ubieto Nogales, Santiago Egea Gomez, Ineke Schuurman, Gorka Labaka, Adrián Núnez-Marcos, Irene Murtagh, Euan McGill, and Horacio Saggion. 2023. SignON: Sign language translation. progress and challenges. In Nurminen, Mary, Judith Brenner, Maarit Koponen, Sirkku Latomaa, Mikhail Mikhailov, Frederike Schierl, Tharindu Ranasinghe, Eva Vanmassenhove, Sergi Alvarez Vidal, Nora Aranberri, Mara Nunziatini, Carla Parra Escartín, Mikel Forcada, Maja Popovic, Carolina Scarton, and Helena Moniz, editors, *Proceedings of the 24th Annual Conference of the European Association for Machine Translation*, pages 501–502, Tampere, Finland, June. European Association for Machine Translation.

Warstadt, Alex, Aaron Mueller, Leshem Choshen, Ethan Wilcox, Chengxu Zhuang, Juan Ciro, Rafael Mosquera, Bhargavi Paranjabe, Adina Williams, Tal Linzen, and Ryan Cotterell, editors. 2023. *Proceedings of the BabyLM Challenge at the 27th Conference on Computational Natural Language Learning*, Singapore, December. Association for Computational Linguistics.

Zhang, Chen, Xiao Liu, Jiuheng Lin, and Yansong Feng. 2024a. Teaching large language models an unseen language on the fly. *arXiv preprint arXiv:2402.19167*.

Zhang, Kexun, Yee Man Choi, Zhenqiao Song, Taiqi He, William Yang Wang, and Lei Li. 2024b. Hire a linguist!: Learning endangered languages with in-context linguistic descriptions. *arXiv preprint arXiv:2402.18025*.

Author Index